D0438165

WAITING AT JOE'S

SEASIDE PUBLISHING

Joe's First Restaurant, painting by Dr. Ferdie Pacheco

WAITING AT

Joe's

DEENY KAPLAN LORBER

Foreword by Larry King

Seaside Publishing

Gainesville · Tallahassee · Tampa · Boca Raton

Pensacola · Orlando · Miami · Jacksonville · Ft. Myers · Sarasota

All photographs are by Adam Lorber.

Printed in the United States of America on recycled, acid-free paper

Library of Congress Cataloging-in-Publication Data
Kaplan Lorber, Deeny, author.
Waiting at Joe's / Deeny Kaplan Lorber ; Foreword by Larry King.
pages cm
ISBN 978-0-942084-09-2 (alk. paper)
    1. Joe's Stone Crab Restaurant—Anecdotes. 2. Restaurants—Florida—
Miami Beach—Employees—Anecdotes. 3. Waiters—Florida—Miami
Beach—Anecdotes. 4. Waitresses—Florida—Miami Beach—Anecdotes.
I. King, Larry, 1933– II. Title.
TX945.5.J647L67 2013
647.95759'381—dc23   2013029220

SEASIDE PUBLISHING

Seaside Publishing is a division of the University Press of Florida.

For a complete list of Seaside books, please contact us:
Seaside Publishing
15 Northwest 15th Street
Gainesville, FL 32611-2079
1-352-392-6867
1-800-226-3822
orders@upf.com
www.seasidepublishing.com

To Adam Balzano, my nephew, who has since passed away

Contents

FOREWORD

If I were asked to name the greatest restaurant I have ever dined in during my seventy-nine years on this planet, it would be, hands down, Joe's Stone Crab.

When I first broke into radio in Miami Beach, in 1957, I was also the track announcer at the Miami Beach Dog Track. It was located right next to Joe's. So every night I would walk past Joe's, look into the window, and wonder if I would ever get to eat there?

Well, things turned out pretty good for me, and I wound up eating there—a lot.

In my opinion, one of the first keys to making it in life is to be seated quickly at Joe's. Jesse Weiss, the son of the original Joe and Jennie, sort of liked me, so all I had to do when I arrived any evening, without calling for a reservation, was nod to the maître d' and walk gently to the bar. And within two minutes, I would hear my name called. This was and is an ongoing thrill.

Once I was having lunch with the GM of the New York Mets, who said, "Why don't we go to Joe's tonight? But you know it's a four hour wait, no matter what."

I responded and quickly said, "I'll tell you what—I bet you we get in in ten minutes. If I'm right, you pay."

He paid.

Once I was in Joe's with my ex-wife Sharon. I was a smoker at the time and suddenly, as we were dining, we smelled smoke.

Everybody in the restaurant that evening smelled smoke. Soon there were firemen throughout Joe's and more firemen on the roof, searching for where the fire was.

As it happened, I was wearing a Pierre Cardin denim outfit, very much the style in those days, and wouldn't you know it, one of *my* cigarette ashes apparently hit the cuff of my pants. I was the fire!

A patron rushed to where we were sitting and spilled water on me. Jesse came over and said, "Only you. Only you, Larry!"

While everybody loved the crabs, I found the veal cutlet out of this world. In fact if you don't order crabs, Joe's is not an expensive restaurant.

I love the waiters, the coffee cups, and the attention to detail. I met so many people there in my young years, including J. Edgar Hoover, baseball great Stan Musial, and George H.W. Bush. There was no place like Joe's in the heyday of Miami Beach. And I never heard anyone speak of a bad meal, or say the wait wasn't worth it.

May it last forever! There will never ever be another spot quite like it.

I remember Jesse Weiss telling me once, "You know, you know, this South Beach area could be big someday, if somebody ever built it up!" Jesse was of course prophetic.

You'll enjoy the stories in this book. Through the eyes of the amazing waiters at Joe's you'll capture the atmosphere that was and is uniquely Joe's.

And here's a tip: always save room for the key lime pie.

Larry King

WAITING AT JOE'S

INTRODUCTION

The World Comes to Joe's

Nat Allen has been waiting at Joe's for forty-six years. A record! That is long enough for him actually to have served the infamous mobster Meyer Lansky, who died in 1983.

Charaff Gouriche came to Joe's by way of an assignment from the king of Morocco.

James "Bones" Jones was forced to leave Miami Beach by curfew, at midnight, or else he would be taken into custody by the local police for the night. When he first started at Joe's more than forty years ago, anyone who was not white was subject to strict "sundown" laws.

Oscar Jimenez grew up in Miami Beach, just across the street from Joe's, but didn't set foot inside the South Beach restaurant until he started working there more than twenty-five years ago.

Janine Ostow told President George W. Bush to wear a bib, and she advised President Clinton that he was going home with her.

Karl "Chopper" Robertson credits Joe's for saving his life—getting him through a tough battle with drug and alcohol dependence in the 1980s. Today he is a manager with a burning loyalty to the restaurant.

Joe's Stone Crab, Miami Beach's oldest restaurant, has provided guests a warm welcome and amazing food since 1913.

A customer wanting cigarettes, in the days before Joe's became a nonsmoking establishment, would simply go across the street. To the curb across the street, because there was always a guy sitting there, loaded with packs of cigarettes.

Many of the waiters used to ride the bus to Miami Beach with a very young Cassius Clay, a.k.a. Muhammad Ali, who was on his way to the 5th Street Gym. Those same waiters were part of the standing ovation when "The Greatest" came to the restaurant for dinner years later.

During World War II the majority of the wait staff at Joe's were women, because so many men were at war.

Joe's Stone Crab, the oldest restaurant in Miami Beach, was established in 1913, when ferries were the only way to get there. Today it is the second highest grossing restaurant in the country, according to Zagat's 2011 restaurant ratings. And the first member of the wait staff was Jennie Weiss—Mrs. Joe, wife of the original Joe Weiss. She set the ground rules for all who followed.

While Joe, an ex-waiter, actually did the cooking, his wife Jennie, an ex-cook, served as the small fish shack's only waiter when they first opened their doors. Role reversals included, this book is all about waiters, then and now. All the Joe's waiters have both a back story and favorite stories to tell about their time waiting at Joe's.

Joe and Jennie's son Jesse learned first-hand what it took to make their restaurant stand out from all others. Today, under the fourth generation of Joe's family, the wait staff make up a large and rather extended family, who work only "in season." (The stone crab season and the restaurant and Take Away season typically starts on October 15 and ends around May 15, with the summer season and menu typically beginning May 29 and ending on or around July 30, after which Joe's closes until the stone crab season resumes in October.) Staff receive three bonuses a year and benefit from a generous profit-sharing plan as well as a 401(k) savings plan. They pay a "barely there" parking permit fee of five dollars a week in Joe's convenient adjacent parking garage. Jo Ann Weiss Sawitz Bass had the idea of expanding the building plans for the multi-level garage, meant to accommodate guests' cars, so that staff could conveniently park on the top floors. Staff also receive a 50 percent discount at Joe's Take Away. And all consider themselves very, very lucky.

Nearly all the waiters with whom I spoke are "lifers," knowing that at Joe's Stone Crab they have landed the very best serving jobs in the industry. They are in it for the long run.

On top of all of that, the waiters' tips are paid on the spot, and if there is a charge card fee involved, Joe's eats the cost.

There are contests of all kinds too: for the waiter who sells

From a fish shack in a spare room of the Weiss family cottage, when the only way to get to Miami Beach was by ferry, Joe's Stone Crab has grown to become a multi-building complex and the second highest grossing restaurant in the United States.

the most crabs that night, the waiter who sells the most daily specials, and so on.

"It is the people who work at Joe's that have made us what we are," explained Jo Ann, who is Joe and Jennie's granddaughter and Jesse's daughter. "We are family, and we all have Joe's best interests at heart."

Today Jo Ann and her son, Stephen Sawitz, oversee the entire venue and every aspect of Joe's daily activity. Jo Ann's daughter, Jodi Hershey, has added to the family legacy as well. There is now a sixth generation that is becoming a part of the legend. As Jodi noted, "Even though my three kids, Jessica,

Lauren and Blayke, have chosen different professions, I know they'd drop everything for Joe's if there was a reason to."

It is not unusual to see Jo Ann clearing tables, wiping up spilled water, or mingling with the customers, many of whom can often be found at Joe's on a daily basis.

Joe's Stone Crab is an amazing one-of-a-kind restaurant that has always been situated at the same location, at the tip of Miami Beach, from the days when its only neighbor was a busy dog track to the hip new landscape: the much-photographed, heavily populated, and ethnically diverse South Beach area of the city, with no sign of the old dog track anywhere.

Joe's was originally known for serving an extremely tasty fish sandwich when it first opened up in a spare room behind Joe and Jennie Weiss's apartment back in 1913, two years before Miami Beach was incorporated. Miami's own native delicacy, and the true star of Joe's, the stone crab, wasn't introduced until 1921.

The sides—coleslaw, grilled tomatoes, creamed spinach, and hash browns—are to die for. The key lime pie is perfect—

Introduced to the menu in 1921, Joe's delicious stone crabs continue to draw guests to the restaurant from around the world.

neither too sweet nor too tart. The quality is always consistent. And even the smartest dressers wear bibs!

Back in 1921 an order of stone crabs cost $.75 for four or five crabs. Potatoes were $.25, and coleslaw sold for $.25 as well. Prices have certainly increased through the years, but the threesome still are regularly sold together and still prepared according to the very same original recipe.

On the occasion of Joe's fiftieth anniversary, stone crabs sold for $4.00, coleslaw sold for $.60, and Lyonnaise potatoes cost $.75. The year was 1963.

By 1978, on Joe's 65th anniversary, stone crabs sold for $6.50, coleslaw sold for $.80 and Lyonnaise potatoes cost $.90.

Today there are four sizes of stone crabs, priced at slightly higher rates, and the prices can vary from day to day due to fishermen's varying costs. At the time of the writing of this book, the costs per order were:

Medium	$28.95
Select	$41.95
Large	$54.95
Jumbo	$79.95

Joe's holds a daily Crab Meeting to discuss the status of the various sizes available of the *Menippe mercenaria*, the succulent Florida stone crabs that Joe Weiss first cooked back in 1921.

Most of the stone crabs caught by Joe's fishermen are found in the Gulf of Mexico. Basically two fisheries, one in Everglades City, Florida, and one in Marathon in the Florida Keys, provide twenty-one boatfuls of the stone crabs daily to Joe's Stone Crab restaurant.

Each morning Chief Operating Officer Stephen Sawitz and staffers Ronnie Pressley and James McClendon take inventory of the number of stone crabs already in house and their respective sizes, and the number of boatfuls due to come in that day,

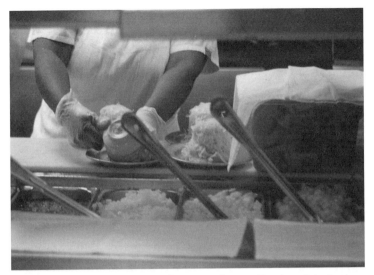

Joe's has evolved with the times, but some things—like the original cole-slaw recipe—are too good to change.

Joe's relies on two Gulf Coast fisheries to provide stone crabs for the an-nual 215-day season. The daily Crab Meeting monitors inventory arriving from twenty-one boats, and Joe's staff has perfected the science and the art of meeting hourly fulfillment of fresh crabs for both onsite and online orders.

and then predict how many will be needed at the day's lunch and dinner. The predictions are based on what was sold on the same day the previous year, pre-orders received overnight from the Shipping department, and early requests from Take Away.

On the day I attended the Crab Meeting, the important countdown to the end of the stone crab season was at 184 days. It is written at the top of each day's crab inventory count. The stone crab season runs for 215 days.

At the beginning Jennie Weiss would rule fiercely over her little establishment. According to her son Jesse's boyhood friend Ralph D. Merritt, there is a story about President Warren G. Harding once coming in with his wife: "The president approached a table and pulled out a chair, but Jennie took the chair away from him, placed it back under the table, and pointed to the side room where her special guests were seated. 'You are in there,' she said, not waiting for a response, and walked back to the kitchen."

To this day Joe's Stone Crab is a restaurant that does not take reservations. Policy has always been "first come, first served," and often a two- to three-hour wait to get seated is the norm.

But this is not a book about waiting to be seated at a table at Joe's Stone Crab. Those reports, I am certain, would amount to millions of individual stories that would probably merit a very big second book.

My focus instead is the waiters on staff—those straight out of the pages of what waiters should be, men and women who have the know-how to turn at least three tables every evening, feeding more than fourteen hundred people on an average night, or a ton of stone crab claws every day. These are waiters who proudly wear the coveted and much respected stone crab lapel pin of gold encrusted embellishment, with faux diamonds. They average about twenty-five years of service at the establishment. All are unique individuals who have worked

Joe's waiters, many of them "lifers," are considered extended family of the landmark institution. Wearing trademark tuxedos, shiny black shoes, stone crab pin, and always a smile, they are the true spirit of Joe's.

very, very hard to secure one of the most sought after food service positions in the business. All seventy-six of them, all waiting at Joe's.

All seventy-six must pass "inspection" every day so as to look their best. They line up in front of their peers to do so. Pressed black tuxedo. Starched tuxedo shirt. Shiny black shoes. Neat and clean appearance. All carrying their tip tray, bread crumber, wine opener, and a stack of menus. It's a parade that is closed to the public but certainly one of the many things that make these waiters truly stand out.

Attention to detail greets celebrities and residents alike and makes Joe's one of Florida's top culinary destinations.

Restaurant food you order, and the wine or cocktails you consume before you reach for your credit card, are among the few purchases that you can actually take advantage of *before* you pay the bill. Think about it. You can't fly on an airplane or wear a new pair of shoes before you pay. But at most restaurants you can order anything you fancy, and enjoy as much of it as you want, and never pay a dime until you are finished.

That's the very reason the staff at Joe's Stone Crab work so hard—they want you to *want* to pay for the special experience of eating a meal "in their home," and they want you to be happy to do so.

Joe's Stone Crab is a Miami Beach institution that has been there for the past hundred years, a go-to epicurean adventure for any visitor, tourist, resident, president, movie star, or gold medal winner.

"And each of the waiters," observed Brian Johnson, the company's general manager and himself a former waiter at Joe's, "has to be extremely MAD to work here." In the language of Joe's, that's the abbreviation for "meticulous at details."

"I worked the floor," Brian explained, starting as a server for the 1980–81 season. "I was the youngest captain at the time, only twenty-four, and figured I'd work here for that one season. And of course, thirty years later, I'm still working at Joe's and loving it. I obviously learned what it took to be really MAD."

"Agreed," said Beverage Director Paul Kozolis, a Joe's staffer since 1979. "What we have here is controlled chaos. In restaurant terms we say that we're happy we are in the weeds—so busy we don't have time to stop, and that's how we like it!"

Former president Clinton and actor Michael Douglas were at Joe's recently, but the attendance of power figures has never

Fresh bread ready to roll—an island of order in the sea of controlled chaos that is service at Joe's Stone Crab.

intimidated any of the employees. Did these celebrity diners wait three hours to be seated? I seriously doubt that. There are exceptions to the waiting rule (which is part of why this book is not about the accepted and expected typical wait to be seated at Joe's).

Did Amelia Earhart, the duke and duchess of Windsor, or actress Gloria Swanson and her secret beau, Joseph P. Kennedy, wait in line? How about Joe DiMaggio, Babe Ruth, J. Edgar Hoover, or Frank Sinatra? Do you think that Al Capone and his gang waited when they arrived daily at 5:00 p.m. for dinner? Probably not. But they did get the star treatment, as do all of Joe's guests—and that's the reason why everybody wants to be a guest at Joe's.

History through the Eyes of the Joe's Waiters

One of Joe's first waiters was Mayberry Kohut, who worked there from 1926 to 1928. In 1985 he wrote Jo Ann Weiss Sawitz Bass a letter:

> In 1926, as a 16-year-old boy, I worked at the Roman Pools, across from the Roney Plaza. Mr. Joe Weiss was there one afternoon and he gave me cards to give to customers—telling them about his place. A week later he hired me to work evenings there. It was a small, white house with 10 tables. There was a picture inside with Mr. and Mrs. Weiss and myself. We had on long white aprons. I waited on Thomas Dewey; James Michener; Joe Kennedy and Gloria Swanson. The best customers, however, were brought to Joe's place by a Colonel Bradley. [Bradley was well known as one of the preeminent owners and trainers of thoroughbred horses in the southern United States during the early twentieth century; he died in August of 1946.]
>
> He owned Bradley Casino, was an investor in the Hialeah Park Race Track on the mainland, and made the cover

of *Time* magazine twice. The Colonel and his gang would often come down to the restaurant around 11 o'clock in the evening, in three white convertible Packards. There were 7 to a car. I would get a $30 tip and Mr. Joe would get a $50 tip. This would happen three nights out of the week. I saved my money to go to Hollywood, California. Joe spent his playing "Clobyosh," a Jewish card game.

The waiters at Joe's Stone Crab today come from more than three dozen nations and speak as many languages. There are married waiters and pregnant waiters. There are second-generation waiters. And siblings. Cousins, too. At one time Chopper Robertson, today a dining room manager, and five of his

Karl "Chopper" Robertson rose through the ranks to become a dining room manager and has trained scores of staff, including five of his own brothers.

brothers were all working at Joe's Stone Crab: Ben, Leroy, John, Craig, and Frank—certainly a family record.

Every night forty-four servers work the tables, and each performs multiple tasks. They first prepare their stations, then they greet their guests, explain the menu, talk about the history of Joe's, take the order, and go to the kitchen to place it. They fetch the order, serve the food, bring the drinks, and clear the tables. Each day every server is given a "side job" to do as well: cleaning the ketchup bottles, filling the saltshakers, and so on.

Waiting at Joe's is demanding, but it is equally rewarding. Not one of the waiters I interviewed ever complained about the demands. They know that the abundance of rewards they receive on a regular basis from working at Joe's are truly the exception to the rule in the waiting game.

Joe's has matured and survived through the century-long history of Miami Beach. The restaurant was born the same year that Carl Fisher arrived, back in 1913, with hopes of bringing to fruition his formidable vision of establishing Miami Beach as a separate and independent city.

Carl Fisher's dream, however, did not include Jews. He refused to sell or rent to most Jews, and Jennie and Joe Weiss were definitely Jewish. Fisher felt that Jews would tarnish his land. Other early developers of Miami Beach felt the same. The Ku Klux Klan marched during that era, underscoring the dramatic climate of prejudice in the new city of Miami Beach. At one point 65 percent of the hotels in Miami Beach, including those owned by Carl Fisher, would not accept Jewish guests.

World War II helped to break down some of the barriers, as U.S. military men of all backgrounds, religions, and races filled the hotels. Many of them were Jews, and many then chose to stay put in the sunshine. By 1947 nearly half of the permanent population of Miami Beach was Jewish.

Joe's has been around from the days when the ferries brought the tourists and would-be customers across the bay, because no freeways, bridges, or causeways had yet been built. The restaurant survived the 1926 hurricane, which destroyed so much of the area; it had to adjust during World War II, when men were at war and women predominated on the wait staff at Joe's, and when the popular Miami Beach hotels were populated by the Army Air Corps right after the attack on Pearl Harbor in 1941.

"Of course, in times of emergency we have contingency plans for the stone crabs," Stephen Sawitz explained. "We need backup in the event of a hurricane, red tide (a harmful marine algae bloom), a strike, inclement weather, long holidays, or if the ocean's predators get too busy." Frozen crabs are prepared by Joe's state-of-the-art fishery especially for occasions like this. And the art of preserving stone crabs (for a limited amount of time, obviously) is a closely guarded Joe's secret.

Following the world war there was a takeover of Miami Beach, when the city became known as a retirement community, with the elder population occupying all the once luxurious beachfront hotels and apartments in the area. Joe's continued through the days when Meyer Lansky and Al Capone made it to their special tables at Joe's, perhaps even on the same evening that J. Edgar Hoover was in the house.

Joe's has thrived through the stories of cocaine and drug wars in the area, when upscale customers flocked to the restaurant, and were then escorted back into their cars right after dinner by off-duty police hired by Joe's, because of the rough and rugged reputation that the area had gained through movies such as *Scarface* and TV shows such as *Miami Vice*.

The establishment then began catering to more of the beautiful people and a new generation of celebrities, with the introduction of the modeling and entertainment industry to South Florida in the early 1990s.

The historic Cuban Mariel boat lift crisis of 1980 brought more Hispanics to Joe's kitchen, where the staff up until that

Keeping in step with the times, Joe's opened a Take Away restaurant, retail outlet, and bistro for folks who want breakfast, or who don't have hours to wait for lunch or dinner.

point had nearly all been African American. That era also brought some of the black kitchen staff to work in the dining room for the first time, or to what is known as the "front of the house."

In this history as told by its long-time wait staff, their memories show how developments at Joe's through the past hundred years have dovetailed with the maturing of the City of Miami Beach, with broader shifts in the country at large, and even with world events. The waiters' profiles are arranged in a loose chronology, reflecting both length of service and key themes in the restaurant's operations.

When my family and I left New York and moved to Miami Beach in 1987, there was still a dress code at Joe's. No shorts, jeans, or cutoffs were allowed, and there were no exceptions whatsoever. Men needed to wear jackets, even for lunch. There was a wardrobe closet beside the maître d's podium at the time, with jackets and dozens of sweatpants for the men and wrap-around skirts for the women.

The current dress code (prominent on the Joe's website, alongside hours and directions) specifies "casual but neat attire": no beach wear, athletic wear, or cutoff shorts, and men must have sleeves.

"Joe's has changed with the times," Stephen Sawitz explained. "And we continue to evolve. The dress code is more lenient today, as shorts and sleeveless tops are acceptable. Our Take Away store, which includes seating for eighty for breakfast, lunch, and dinner as well, adjacent to the restaurant, is a perfect example. We have needed to meet the lifestyle of our customers. Not everyone has the time to wait in line. So now you can place your order over the Internet, call it in, or just stop by to view the very fresh stone crabs, variety of colorful salads, or sumptuous baked goods—and that quickly, your dinner is ready. You can even come in for breakfast."

Not only do guests come to Joe's from all over the world, but the Joe's Stone Crab products are shipped nationally, via online orders and overnight shipping.

Tony Marquez manages the growing Shipping department, which will soon have its own building in the complex.

Besides the world coming to Joe's, the fare goes out to the world as well. Stone crabs are now shipped anywhere in the continental United States. And the future for this part of the Joe's business continues to expand every year. "Soon we're going to have a building nearby that will be built just for our Shipping department," Jo Ann explained proudly. Joe's Take Away and Shipping departments have made it easy for anyone, almost anywhere, to enjoy its world-renowned menu.

Breakfast at Take Away offers a South Beach omelet, for example, consisting of eggs, spinach, feta cheese, and of course stone crab meat. When the idea for the Take Away first came about, Jo Ann handed the task over to her children. It was an assignment that members of the fourth generation of Joe's immediate family, Jodi and Stephen, gladly pursued in order to bring their own new vision to the new generation of Joe's patrons.

"People didn't want to wait in line. Not everyone had the time to wait," Jodi Hershey explained. "So Take Away, even with a simple menu back then, became an instant success!"

The Joe's complex now consists of four separate businesses: the restaurant itself, Take Away, Wholesale, and Shipping. Take Away today offers Joe's own private wine label, items for the gourmet cook and kitchen, fresh flowers, and the ability to plan an entire meal from appetizers to dessert.

There are certain times of the year when the Shipping department or Take Away actually outsells the restaurant. According to Jose Uchuya, Joe's dining room manager, "last New Year's Eve, Take Away outsold the restaurant. Of course that didn't come as a surprise, and the staff trained all year to be able to provide every customer with as many stone crabs and as much key lime pie as they would want on that very special evening."

Shipping too, according to Jose, continues to break records. "Well, it makes sense if you think about it. The restaurant is bound to the amount of seats we have. Take Away and Shipping, however, can see one person buy enough food for fifty people in just ten minutes! In the restaurant, to serve fifty people, you're looking at over two hours to do the same thing!"

The staff at Take Away, adjacent to the main dining room, are able to become Joe's waiters too. An example is Kiera Henry, whom you'll meet in this book, still referred to as a "newbie" with just ten years of waiting at Joe's under her belt.

"Yes," Jose added. "We used to have cross training, where our dining room waiters would work in Take Away over the summer [Take Away is now closed over the summer, but Shipping is open during the off season]. It was always a win-win. They made extra money, and we had seasoned servers, who knew our menu inside-out, working with another in-house department."

Through the years, Joe's has maintained some inexpensive items on its menu specifically so that anyone can afford to come in for a meal. One couple, according to several of the waiters, has been eating at Joe's once a week for the past fifty years. They order iced tea and split an order of fried chicken and coleslaw, and their bill has never been higher than $17.50. Jo Ann will not raise the prices. "For all the years they've been coming here, they've helped me to pay my mortgage," Joe's proud matriarch explained. "I'm just glad they keep coming."

1

THE VOICE ON THE MICROPHONE

Or, Joe's First Chance to Make an Impression

1

ED WITTE

As usual on a busy night of the week at Joe's, the wait reaches far beyond the elegant foyer, past the strikingly handsome mahogany bar installed to serve those waiting in line for a table, and out into the open courtyard, where comfortable garden chairs and tables accommodate Joe's waiting guests.

As guests approach the podium upon their arrival, a tuxedo-clad gentleman takes the name of their party and predicts a nearly 100 percent accurate wait time for them. "Of course we'll try to get them in before the promised time, and make them feel even more special by doing so," said Ed.

There have been other men on that microphone before him as head maître d'—among them Roy Garret and Dennis Sutton—calling out the names as the tables became ready for their guests, but tonight the voice is Ed's. How did he get there? He started his journey at Joe's as a waiter, and this is his story.

New Jersey born, Ed Witte hadn't even heard of Joe's Stone Crab when he first came to visit his dad in South Florida during spring break in 1991. "I had been attending college at Penn State and Rutgers when I came to visit. I really wasn't happy at school. I was restless. I wanted to move on with my life. So I told my dad I didn't want to go back to school, and he then promptly told me to get a job."

With some serving experience in his teens, the young architectural student with the curious mind listened to the

Joe's waiting guests are served from a handsome mahogany bar and can enjoy garden seating in the courtyard.

suggestion of his father. He was told to knock on the doors of two South Florida institutions to look for work: Burt & Jack's in Fort Lauderdale and Joe's Stone Crab in Miami Beach.

"I hadn't heard of either, and apparently I made the right choice. Burt & Jack's has been out of business for years," Ed commented. (The steakhouse opened in 1984 and closed in 2002.)

He learned from a friend that Joe's allows only one day each year to be dedicated to the hiring of new (but experienced) wait staff. The friend who suggested he go for an interview was also a friend of Calvin Keel's brother; Calvin was the kitchen manager at Joe's for more than fifty years.

Typically the interviews are held on the second Tuesday in October, and the annual event has come to be known as Roll Call. It's mostly based on word of mouth, although also advertised in the *Miami Herald*, and is basically an open call for servers and a tradition well known through the local food server community. It usually attracts more than a hundred applicants, all vying for a limited number of open server slots.

"When I went to the Roll Call back in 1991, I was only twenty years old," Ed recalled fondly. "But I came with a lot of server experience, and since it's widely known that Joe's does *not* train waiters—that you must come with experience—I knew I had that going for me. I was confident that I had what it would take!"

Roll Call is today conducted by three members of Joe's wait staff, and each applicant is required to take and pass what insiders call a "tray test."

"Yes, this part of the interview and test can eliminate an applicant right away," Ed explained. It involves lifting and carrying a loaded and very heavy serving tray. Waiting at Joe's can be physically demanding. "In fact it is quite obvious that during their down time, many of the Joe's waiters generally put on

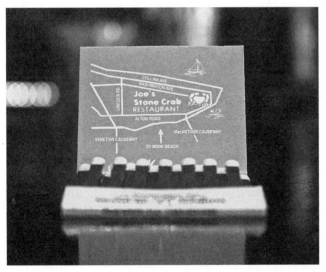

Opened two years before Miami Beach was incorporated, Joe's was originally known for its fish sandwich. The 1920s saw the region's native delicacy of stone crab added to the menu, and Joe's survived a 1926 hurricane to become a beloved local fixture.

a few pounds, as carrying the tray does require a tremendous discipline and the heavy lifting can keep the weight off."

As one would imagine, given the inviting job conditions already described, the number of server positions to be filled during each annual Roll Call is limited due to the extremely low turnover. Joe's kitchen workers have applied for Roll Call as well, and if they make it, they have the benefit of already having seniority over any of the newcomers.

"We try to keep it in the family," Jo Ann Weiss Sawitz Bass added. "If we can promote, we do. Oscar Jimenez, for example, worked as a crab cracker in the kitchen for years, and then became a busser and then a server."

And once you've made it through the Roll Call you typically have to work five shifts at lunch, for three years, in order to become a night waiter, the goal of any of Joe's wait staff. Nights are where the money is.

Ed had a birthday before starting his new job. But even with the cockiness and the I-can-do-attitude of a wide-eyed lad of twenty-one, the first day on the job for the youngest of Joe's waiters wasn't without anxiety.

The first three days are set aside for "trailing," when the new waiter shadows an experienced waiter to see if he or she has what it takes. This is where strengths and weaknesses really come through.

"So I was asked if I knew how to open a bottle of champagne," Ed recalled, "and of course I said, 'Sure.' Well, I popped the cork and instantaneously that champagne was all over my shoes, foaming like there was no tomorrow. Jo Ann, my new boss, was right there. Right there! She saw it all. But she also saw that I knew how to handle the situation. And that was the key. Knowing how to focus when things go the wrong way—that's part of what it takes!"

According to Ed, it's all about good food and good service. "A waiter has maybe three to four minutes with each guest to make an impression. My job is always to make our guests feel

Meet the voice on the microphone, Ed Witte. Formerly an architecture student and now head maître d', Ed launches guests into their Joe's experience with a warm greeting and—eventually—the call to seating.

special, to feel unique as soon as they walk in the door and up to the podium to give me their name and the number of people in their party. I believe that is what sets Joe's apart. And it's the same with the waiters. They want to make every one of their guests feel special too."

Less than a year after becoming a Joe's waiter, Ed was asked to become a seating captain for the lunch hour guests. Still serving at dinnertime, Ed found he was inching more and more into the position of a true Joe's cheerleader.

"I never even heard of stone crabs when I first came to Florida, but now I can't get enough," Ed added. "And the ginger salmon is one of my favorite things on the menu. I strongly recommend that you try everything on our menu. It's all amazing!

"I love visiting other restaurants with my wife Lori on my days off, because I've never found even one restaurant that can compare in any way to Joe's."

Before each shift, the waiters at Joe's are asked to arrive about an hour and a half early, to share a "family" meal, discuss the day's specials, and learn about new menu items or any pressing issues. That's when the daily inspection of the waiters takes place as well.

"This is the very best way to maintain a cohesive team spirit," Ed observed, "and keep everyone at the top of their game. We all very much enjoy this part of each working shift—getting together for a meal and even the inspection. It's a bridge between what happens outside the restaurant in our diverse private lives and the time when we begin to represent the Joe's family each day, being the very best at what we do, as one winning team."

From a role as part-time lunch seating captain, Ed quickly became a part-time maître d', and for the past six years he has donned a tuxedo every night and has become "The Voice," the head maître d' at Joe's.

The maître d', of course, is to be celebrated. Every Joe's regular, and anyone else in the know, will usually make sure that the legendary exit handshake with this particular person includes a thank you and a generous tip. An assurance that the next time you come in, you'll be remembered.

II

AND THE WAITERS
WHO WAIT

2

NAT ALLEN

Forty-six years! That's how long Nat Allen has been a fixture at Joe's Stone Crab. Almost half a century. The history and the memories and stories that live within Nat can be somewhat overwhelming.

Raised in Alabama, Nat followed his older sister to Miami back in 1960. "There was just no work in Alabama at the time, and I needed to work." He was in the eleventh grade.

His first job was at Wolfie's, a popular deli then located a couple of miles to the north of Joe's. "I was a porter, a cook and a busser. And then I met Calvin Keel, who everyone knew ran Joe's kitchen."

Nat first met Calvin shooting pool, which was part of the after-hours black culture during those days, "and he asked me to come to Joe's for an interview. You had to know someone to get that interview," Nat recalled.

Calvin Keel was definitely *the* person to know back then, especially for a young black man. Calvin worked at Joe's for fifty years, from 1958 to 2008. After speaking to Calvin, Nat Allen was hired, serving as a busser from 1966 until 1992 and becoming head busman along the way.

During that time he had children and needed more money. He began working two jobs, the second as a plumber/electrician, but Nat really wanted to remain a full-time Joe's employee.

Having started as a busser in 1966, Nat Allen is the elder statesman among many long-term waiters and has enjoyed relationships with regulars such as J. Edgar Hoover.

"In 1992 I got tired of working two jobs. It was killing me. I wanted to be a Joe's waiter, a full-time waiter," he reflected. "And I learned how to be a good waiter all on my own. I watched the good ones for a long time and I knew I had exactly what it takes."

He asked, and he got the job.

J. Edgar Hoover used to come in and Nat would serve him coffee. Nat and the FBI chief became friendly. "He was so colorful," Nat recalled. "I really enjoyed our time together."

Muhammad Ali became a buddy. "I met him when I visited one of my friends at the 5th Street Gym, which was walking distance from Joe's. And years later, when Ali walked into Joe's for dinner—well, I had never seen anything like it. The entire restaurant got up and applauded as he walked across the room to his table. That was the respect he got. That was the kind of man he was! It was an unbelievable tribute."

Back when Nat first started working at Joe's in the 1960s, the waiters from Wolfie's, Pumpernicks, Joe's, and other establishments used to unwind after work by meeting at clubs across the bay, like the Rocky Palace at 2nd Avenue and 9th Street, or Harlem Square at 2nd and 10th. "We all knew each other. Everyone used to stop by. Even Ali."

These after-hours hangouts were in Overtown, a hub for late-night gathering and entertainment at the time. And it wasn't just blacks who frequented the sultry nightspots; the white upper crust came too.

It was still the era when big-time entertainers like Sammy Davis Jr., Count Basie, and Ella Fitzgerald would perform at the fancy hotels of Miami Beach but then were not allowed to stay the night because of the color of their skin. "So they'd cross the bay and party in Overtown. And all of us would party with them," Nat explained. There was a curfew in Miami Beach for people of color, and any after-hours activities had to be on the Miami side of Biscayne Bay.

"There was another spot called the Fiesta, where groups like Sam & Dave, and just about anyone you could imagine, used to perform. We'd all meet and have a great time," he recalled with fondness for a vibrant and exciting era long gone. "Those are great memories and were part of the culture back then," he added, "but they are only memories now."

Was segregation part of Joe's past? It is doubtful. Joe's did, however, have two distinct sides of the house: the kitchen side was referred to as the back of the house, and the waiters were known as the front. The kitchen staff were all black. The servers were all white. The front of the house used the toilet closer to the dining room. The kitchen staff used the toilet closer to where they were. Was it segregation? No one I spoke with thought so. It's just how things were.

Nat abandoned early dreams of becoming a pilot, but life is good for the oldest Joe's employee. "My children and grand-children mean everything to me. And when I'm not at Joe's we are together. I'm pretty lucky."

"I love everything on the menu," Nat added. "When I was at home on the farm, all of the food we ate was home grown. I learned to eat everything—and between my mother's kitchen and Joe's kitchen, I can say that I've never had a bad meal!"

3

James Jones, a.k.a. "Bones" or JT

The year 2012 marked Bones's fortieth anniversary at Joe's. The long-time Joe's employee and the establishment share a lot of history

Raised on a farm in southwest Georgia with seven brothers and sisters, Bones knew, even as a teen, that there was only so much you could do, only so far you could go, living on a farm in Georgia.

So he moved to Miami, to his aunt's attic. She happened to live next door to the guy who made the key lime pie at Joe's, a man named Paul Wilson Sr. "I hadn't heard of key lime pie, and I certainly hadn't heard of Joe's," Bones recalled, "but I needed a job."

The big guy started his career at Joe's washing pots, and that lasted three weeks: "I wasn't very good at it." This was in April of 1972, and the next move for the ex–farm boy was as a dishwasher in Joe's kitchen. "And I was pretty good at that," Bones added. "I thought I'd found my calling."

It turned out that he knew some of the busboys from back home, and Calvin Keel, the kitchen manager, saw him helping them out by carrying their trays of dirty dishes back into the kitchen. He was very good at it. The trays were heavy and awkward, but Bones had a knack for it.

James "Bones" Jones, or JT, has spent more than forty years at Joe's, advancing from dishwasher to dining room captain, and shares his memories of Miami Beach as a "sundown" town, when African Americans could be jailed if seen on the streets after curfew.

"One night, out of the blue, Calvin asked me if I had a pair of black pants and a white shirt," he recalled fondly, "and of course I said yes, and before I knew it, I had officially become a busboy and said goodbye to the kitchen."

For nineteen years Bones was a busboy, which then became known as busman, and eventually he was made head busser.

Things were different then for the bussers, according to Karl "Chopper" Robertson. "There was a lot of drinking on the premises. As soon as the customers would leave the table, the bussers would rush over and grab the wine bucket and finish whatever was in the bottle! That wouldn't happen today, but back then, it was how it was.

"All of the fun aside, we certainly did well in tips," Bones observed, "bringing in at least 15 percent of what the waiters made. I was very happy." This was a generous salary for any career busser.

"But through the years, I did take interest in the captain's job. I learned exactly what it was about—I got to watch them work every day. I knew I could do it. I asked for the job three times. It took me asking three times, but I eventually landed the job and I love it."

Bones's first quest to become a captain resulted in: "You need to leave and get some experience somewhere else in being a captain." But he didn't want to leave.

His second quest to become a captain was likewise rebuffed. "Again, they told me I needed experience to be considered."

By the third time, Bones went to the woman he knew would listen. He knew he was ready. He'd had plenty of time to study what it takes to be a captain at Joe's.

"I spoke with Jo Ann and I told her what had transpired so far. She immediately picked up the phone and called down from her office above the dining room and asked why I couldn't have the job. Well, the next thing I knew, she was giving me money to buy two tuxedos. Just like that, I had the job.

"I did tell her that I very much wanted the job and thanked her, but at the same time I also told her I didn't need the money. I could afford the suits," he laughed.

Bones became the daytime captain and today is the dining room captain and also a maître d', working closely with Ed Witte. Bones, or JT, may seem a daunting figure, but his considerable stature and big bright smile make him one of the most recognized members on the Joe's team today, and I believe one of the most loved as well.

"I like being the dining room captain. When Ed's back is to the dining room as he welcomes our customers, my job is to make sure that each of them leaves happy, to make sure the restaurant is covered and that our staff all do their jobs.

"Working at Joe's is a tough job," Bones commented, "because our standards are so high. Our kitchen has to be as clean as our dining room. Our people have to look their best."

Over the forty years that Bones has been part of the Joe's family, things certainly have changed a lot. "There was nothing south of 5th Street back then and almost no competition. There were no other restaurants in the area. And there was that midnight curfew on Miami Beach for many of us," he recalled.

Bones tells the story of taking the jitney over the bay from Biscayne Boulevard on the mainland, "and that jitney wasn't allowed to go further than 5th and Alton Road at the time. We had to walk the rest of the way.

"And if we were out past curfew, the cops would have to bring us in, hold us overnight, and then let us go the following morning," he added. That was the law. Miami Beach back then, just forty years ago, was still what was referred to as a "sundown" town. No blacks were allowed on the streets after sundown.

"One night because I was working late here at Joe's, I missed the jitney to go home and came back and found Jesse Weiss smoking a cigar on the porch," said Bones with a big smile on his face. "What a guy he was. Understanding the situation right away, he immediately called the chief of police, his good friend Rocky Pomerance, who personally brought his car to pick me up and drive me across the bay to Biscayne Boulevard. It was a different time."

If you wanted to make money, you worked for it, Bones explained. "I used to make it a point to remember even the little things, the type of bread a customer liked, or if he liked it warm. It's those things that brought in big tips. And $5 back then was considered a very big tip." A Super Bowl dinner once yielded the big guy a memorable $500 tip. "But each time, no matter who it may be, or how big the bill was, you work for your tips."

Everyone seems to know Bones. "I think they know me by word of mouth, and I always try to make them feel special." As far as I could ascertain, no one has ever said a bad word about this gentle giant.

Bones's favorite customer, believe it or not, was "The Fonz"—the iconic Arthur Herbert Fonzarelli of the 1970s sitcom *Happy Days*, played by Henry Winkler. "He came here twice, and each time he was by himself. He called me a cool dude. I like that. And I liked Brooke Shields too. She was married to André Agassi at the time and she hugged me. She said I smelled like her dad—we both wore Old Spice. I didn't even know who she was, but I sure liked the hug!"

Bones is a big Dol-phan and loves tailgating at Dolphins football games. "It's my time to hang out with the boys." He is a private person but admits to playing tight end, was a linebacker in school, "and when I first came to Miami I joined a league in Overtown." The Overtown section of Miami, across the bay from Miami Beach, was a black community. Much of it was destroyed when a section of the city's main highway was constructed back in 1961: Route I-95 that now leads all roads to Miami Beach.

Bones has raised three children, each of whom has a master's degree today. Not bad for a farm boy from Georgia.

His cousin Moses is also a Joe's waiter.

"I think the biggest change in my forty years at Joe's, besides what's developed south of 5th Street, is the kitchen. The food. The presentation of the food. The variety of what we serve today. Everything is made to order now. It's why our reputation continues to grow every year and I am so proud to be a part of this exceptional family.

"Jo Ann is the fairest person I've ever met in my life and she always does the right thing. Joe's is the best, because of what she gives to everyone on a daily basis," Bones concluded. "She sets the standard for all of us."

4

MIKE FRANK, A.K.A. "PHILLY" OR "TRAVELING MIKE"

"There were three Mikes when I came to Joe's nearly thirty years ago, back in 1983. So they asked me what my middle name was, but there was another David. My last name is Frank. And you got it, there was already a waiter named Frank. I was from Philadelphia, and they started calling me Philly and—well, I've been known as Philly ever since."

He's also known as Traveling Mike, because whenever he has a chance, he travels.

"I still travel the same way. I've been to 135 countries and all 50 states. And I'm still backpacking. If it doesn't fit in my backpack, it doesn't come along," Philly explained. "At first I was off five months a year (before Joe's offered a summer menu and summer hours). Now it's two, and I still take advantage of every minute that I'm not working. I'd give myself a $10,000 budget, or $60 per day, when I had five months, limiting myself to a $1,000 airfare bill, and I was off."

Joe's gave the wayward traveler an opportunity to pursue his dreams. With a political science degree from Philadelphia's Temple University, he's now become expert in worldwide politics, a definite conversation point when greeting his international clientele at Joe's. And Philly proudly shared his checked

Having backpacked through 135 countries, Mike "Philly" Frank shares his experiences with Joe's international clientele and still pursues his travel passion during his two months off every year.

list of places traveled, clearly about two thirds of the world's surface! Quite impressive.

"A friend of mine was getting married in Miami. I came down. I felt the weather. I thought that I would be an idiot if I stayed up North, so Miami became home.

"I came to Joe's with a lot of bartending experience, because I worked my way through school," Traveling Mike explained. "I was a political junkie and I first traveled in the summer of 1972. I haven't stopped since, and Joe's has given me the opportunity to continue that dream."

When he first came to Miami he hadn't even heard of Joe's. "I worked at so many places before I came here," he reminisced. "The Cricket Club, The Forge. I was at the Cricket Club, when

Marina Polvay, food consultant to Al Malnik, who owned both restaurants, suggested that I go to work at The Forge."

"I applied at Joe's for a bartending position, but none was available. I therefore applied for the wait staff vacancy. By that time there were a lot of ex-Forge waiters waiting at Joe's.

Philly came to Joe's and made the cut, and it's been a love affair ever since.

He still travels whenever he can but has developed a new passion that rules much of his off time today. "I have found that I love cooking, and fortunately the two do go hand in hand. I travel and I learn about foods around the world."

Philly makes a mean homemade spicy pickle and smooth, yummy hummus, two of my favorites.

"I have fun with my guests," Philly concluded. "Ali is one of my favorites. And Madonna has been at my table too. She came in at the time that her bustiers were making news. She faced the window and had bodyguards all around her. She took off her jacket and was obviously cold. Real cold. All over cold!

"I wanted to tell her that she was inappropriately dressed, but she was Madonna, so I did what I could to make her comfortable. I remember that she wanted crab cakes. No problem. But I did bring her some stone crabs too. I know she had a good time.

"I get to experience other good restaurants when I travel and usually go during lunch, as the menu is far less expensive." Philly laughed as he continued, "And there is no place like Joe's. None of the places I've been to, anywhere in the world, can compare to what we have here at Joe's. I have become a sort of travel and food consultant for a lot of my guests. They ask me where to go in cities around the globe, and of course, it is my pleasure to assist."

5

JANINE OSTOW

She's a New Yorker, part Italian, part Jewish, and it shows. Armed with the chutzpa for waiting confidently on the most demanding guests at Joe's, the gutsy server is often the one who is called upon to serve the restaurant's most famous, infamous, and intimidating guests.

"To be asked to serve some of the elite by my peers is one of the highest compliments I could ever receive," Janine smiled.

This is Janine's twentieth season at Joe's. "I come from the Bronx. When I was twelve my family moved to Miami Beach," she explained. "I got into the restaurant biz because I thought it would be fast cash—easy money."

Janine came to a mini Roll Call that took place in February, because there was a shortage of servers during lunch. She had worked in other restaurants before; she knew you had to come to Joe's with experience, and made the cut because she was well qualified.

"But it was daunting at first."

One of fifteen women on the floor today, Janine has an allegiance to Joe's and all of its members. "You have seventy brothers and sisters for most of the year, and I believe we all really have each other's backs."

She recalled her early days: "There was no air conditioning in the kitchen. We garnished our own food. We did everything back then. I saw the older guys doing it all and knew that I could too."

Back in 1991 the Equal Employment Opportunity Commission took Joe's to court. The case revolved around the idea that between 1986 and 1990 Joe's hired no female servers. Looking through the case records, however, it becomes evident that the management staff of Joe's at the time were almost all women; there were women in the kitchen; and there were women waiters on the floor.

"The truth is that very few women ever came to Roll Call, and if they didn't come, there certainly wasn't a chance of their being hired," Janine observed. "And some of those same women who testified in the suit hadn't ever applied for a position at Joe's. If they had, they would have recalled the tray test—because there are many men who can't pass the demanding test either."

Chopper Robertson agreed. "It is difficult, even for the men, to lift a twenty- to twenty-five-pound loaded tray with one arm. Janine is one of the women who can!"

According to Robertson, when carrying the tray, you cannot have anything in the other hand whatsoever: "It's a balance thing, and another layer of protection in the event that someone may be off balance."

"And don't forget that through the years, Joe's has experienced an extremely low turnover," Janine added. "You don't leave Joe's unless you are dead." All the waiters I interviewed for this book pretty well agreed on that.

Working steadily five nights a week today, Janine always makes sure she is available if she needs to fill in at lunch as well.

"We have early and late shifts too," she explained. "The early shift calls for an arrival time of 3:30 p.m. If you come in early, you make sure your station and your partner's station are ready. You do the side work (cleaning the salt and pepper and such) for both stations too. So if you're on late shift, which means you arrive at 4:30, the following week you and your partner switch off."

As noted, Janine is often the server who is called on to welcome the most famous of Joe's guests.

"I first met President Clinton at a fundraiser that Joe's was involved in at a beautiful neighborhood called Cocoplum, in South Miami. There were twelve of us. He was so gracious and sincere. After dinner he took pictures with the entire group. I somehow managed to have a shot of just him and me as well.

"And then a few years later we were told that he would be coming in to Joe's for dinner. Everyone knew I had that picture of me with President Clinton, and at their consistent urging, I brought it in and hung it up in the back room where he and his party would be eating.

"I was one of the servers for the president's group that night. Well, after dinner, when I thought Mr. Clinton was leaving, I started taking the picture down. He walked right up to me and looked at me funny, and I looked at him and said, 'Sir, you *are* going home with me tonight.' And you bet, he laughed big time!"

With President George W. Bush, Janine's chutzpa was put to the test again. "It was the last day of the summer season. Jeb Bush was with his brother, and actor Andy Garcia was in their party as well.

"I welcomed everyone and offered them a typical Joe's meal—stone crabs, grilled tomatoes, garlic spinach, hash browns. But Jeb wanted something else. The president said, 'I'm going with whatever she says!'"

Janine even had her own Secret Service agent that evening, assigned to tail her every move. "Jeb wanted coleslaw and for some reason I couldn't find my partner. My tray was full, and I really didn't want to keep the president and his party waiting. Since the Man in Black was by my side every step of the way, making sure the food I brought to the table was safe, I asked him to help me carry the second tray. And he was so flustered, he did! Everyone was shocked at the sight of the Secret Service agent carrying a heavy tray to the table, and when they realized what was going on, they all applauded.

"Each time I came back to the East Wing where the president and his party were seated, I had to go through a metal scanner. It was annoying to them and to me.

"After several scans, I took out my keys, since the alarm kept going off, and put them on the table directly in front of the president and his party. And as I did so, I quickly said, 'Gentlemen, anything that I find missing from my car or home tonight, you are in big trouble.'"

Needless to say, Janine was a successful and entertaining host.

"So I brought out the bibs that same night and began to put them on my guests. The president said, "Do you really think I need this?' And I said, 'Sir, you are in my house tonight, and I make the rules.' He cracked up and he *did* wear his bib!"

TV and movie stars also sit with Janine. "Ann-Margret and her husband Roger Smith came in once and sat at my station. Well, I know I can get sassy, but this one just rolled off my tongue. I asked Mr. Smith if he wanted anything, and he said: 'I'm good.' And I came right back with, 'I know you are good, Mr. Smith, but can I bring you something to drink?'"

Janine's favorite celebrity guest: actress and Emmy® Award winner Sharon Gless, who now lives on Miami Beach. Sharon absolutely considers Janine Ostow one of the best.

Sharon is currently starring in the USA series *Burn Notice*, shot locally in Miami, and she and her husband, producer Barney Rosenzweig, are frequent Joe's guests.

Sharon is generous, often bringing gifts to her favorite people, and Janine certainly is one of them.

"The day Janine and I met at Joe's, we hit it off. I really love Janine because of her irreverence—she is so wonderfully rude to me," the blonde TV icon explained. "With Janine, I never stop laughing. I count on her to be rude. Respectfully rude! She

Janine Ostow—pictured here with one of Joe's biggest fans, Emmy® Award–winning actress Sharon Gless—is an equal opportunity joker, serving up generous helpings of wit with the crabs she serves her guests, no matter how famous they may be.

knows she can throw anything at me, and she does. Janine has *the* most amazing wit. I love her brilliant sense of humor. I am drawn to her warmth."

Janine is a big *Burn Notice* fan. Sharon responds accordingly: "We are shooting our seventh season, and every year I bring Janine a show t-shirt—after I wear it. That is her detailed prerequisite. I have to have worn it before giving it to her. Of course, I always wash it first.

"And of course, Janine can produce miracles. The final day of the season last year, when the kitchen was winding down for summer break, Barney wanted something. Janine said she thought they were out of whatever it was he wanted, and then excused herself. Well, it seems that someone else had ordered the last of whatever it was—but Janine somehow came through. She said, 'Just don't ask. Just enjoy it!'"

Yes, Janine would go to the ends of the earth to make sure her guests get what they really want. Her stories are many, and she can even be credited with feeding Shaquille O'Neal his first stone crab.

"I love making our guests happy," Janine explained. "If I can go home at the end of the day and know that I made someone's day, then I'm pretty happy too."

6

JIMMY AGOSTINHO

"I am Portuguese, but I was raised, the youngest of a very large family, in Springfield, Massachusetts.

"The dream of every member of my family in Springfield was to learn a trade (college was never in the picture), make enough for a downpayment for a duplex that would bring in money to help pay the mortgage, find a wife, and live happily ever after," Jimmy explained.

Working at first in a diner in Massachusetts, the young Jimmy was befriended by the owner, who suggested he go to Miami and earn the $10,000 he needed for a downpayment on that duplex. Jimmy's new boss had a cousin who lived there and suggested that Jimmy go to stay with him while banking the money.

At first Jimmy worked at other restaurants in the area, but everyone, it seems, took a liking to the young man, and several suggested that he use his skills at Joe's. "I checked it out and saw that they were expanding, and I learned that they had a great reputation. I saw myself as part of that expansion. It became my new dream."

Jimmy didn't get hired at first, but he knew someone who worked at Joe's, and did get the job shortly after his first attempt.

"I thought I would eventually go back to my large family and pursue the dream that everyone else I knew was after, but I

Growing up in a trade-oriented Portuguese family, Jimmy Agostinho pursued his own version of the American dream, setting roots in Miami. He now sees his children following the same path, with a son headed to medical school.

never went home. I liked being on my own," Jimmy reflected. "At the beginning, I thought I'd make enough in that first year at Joe's to go home and put that downpayment on a duplex—but I was happy in Miami Beach and at Joe's. I had a new home and found I was pursuing a different dream.

"Waiting at Joe's is not just a job. You can make a really good living here," he continued. "You need to be the best you can be, and then you are a king. I'm even a kind of celebrity now when I go home to visit," he laughed. "They are all jealous that I only work seven months a year!" [Waiters can choose to work only in the October 15–May 15 stone crab season or work the summer season as well.]

"I found my own dream, because of what Joe's has given me. I invested in a cottage in Maine. It'll be my retirement one day. And I found a wife, here in Miami. We have twins. A boy and a girl. A perfect family," said Jimmy proudly.

With his son soon heading off to medical school, it was clear that the family's tradition of learning a trade and not even considering college was long gone. "My children have inherited our family work ethic, however. I'm so proud of that."

Like many of his colleagues, Jimmy has an artistic side as well. He's an artist. He creates sculptures and beautiful inlaid, hand-carved wooden boxes that are perfection, with such detail and passion.

This marks Jimmy's twenty-eighth season waiting at Joe's. He's also a captain at lunch and at dinner. "Through those years I've had opportunities to see my customers' families grow; I really got to know them, and they me. Sometimes it's sad when one of my regulars is brought to the table in a wheelchair, and you know that this may be the very last time you see them. But that's what Joe's gives you. We have the ability to meet and truly get to know so many wonderful people.

"When I first started at Joe's, with the old dining room arrangement, the maître d' saw everything. He was situated in the front of the restaurant and watched everything flow. He was like a conductor. He always knew when a table was about to become empty, and always had the next party waiting. Today, with our renovation and the many dining room areas, the captains all have become the eyes of the maître d', and things have continued to run smoothly and quite seamlessly."

Caring for customers is the watchword. And what if a guest has one too many? "We can cut off a customer and stop someone from having another drink. We're all taught to use the right terminology. To be cautious."

7

KEVIN MURPHY

It's been twenty-eight years for Kevin Murphy. He came to Miami from his native Winchester, Massachusetts, when he was only twenty-one. That was back in 1976.

"My first job in Florida was at the Newport Hotel. A friend of mine got me the job. The Newport had a very young clientele, and the goal there was to keep everyone at the resort, so there were always all sorts of activities going on. I worked my way up, and by the end of my third year I became superintendent of service for the hotel."

It was actor Frank Fontaine's son, Jackie, who first suggested the Newport to his friend Kevin. "Remember Frank, a well-known comedian who was famous for his Crazy Guggenheim character back in the '60s? Jackie Fontaine and I have been friends since we were kids.

"After a few years, I wasn't sure that this was really the career path I wanted to take, so I got a job selling cars at Tropical Chevrolet, just north of downtown Miami. That was in 1979. Gas prices were high. Interest rates were high. No one was buying. This was clearly a bad decision."

After a year Kevin headed back to the Newport, but he now knew he wanted to work on the other side, in the restaurants. He began as a server, became good, and then moved to a more upscale establishment, La Paloma on Biscayne Boulevard.

Kevin Murphy has experienced first-hand the way Joe's takes care of its family. Giving away his own coveted crab lapel pin to supermodel Elle McPherson, when she was a guest at his station, was double the pleasure for Kevin—knowing that monies from crab pin sales at Joe's are used for employee emergencies and charitable donations and that he was able to purchase another.

"Back in 1982 La Paloma was hot! [It was in its infancy then and is now closed.] It was mobbed every night. I spent over two years there as a server."

One day Kevin visited Joe's to see his friend Glen, whose brother Dennis Sutton was at one time the head maître d' at Joe's. At this point, however, the head maître d' was Roy Garret.

"According to Roy, there were no positions available. But I came in again a week later, and Roy told me that there was an opening. I jumped," Kevin recalled. "That was back in March of '84."

Unlike other Joe's waiters, who would start at lunch and work their way into nights, Kevin Murphy began his career at Joe's working five nights on the floor.

"Guess I was in the right place at the right time, as the saying goes. I also lucked out because Dotty Malloy [see part III], who happened to be the only female server at the time, really took me under her wing. I had just met her, but she would introduce me to everyone as her nephew."

By 1987 Kevin became a lunch captain, working with Anthony Arneson, whose story follows. Today he remains a lunch captain two days a week and works nights five days a week.

At the beginning of his tenure at Joe's, Kevin would take a job during the summer months at Houston's. "I did that for three years. The system was so different there. The staff were all transients. Nice people, but basically students, working part-time. The expectations were so different. The experience made me appreciate what Joe's was all about.

"If you take a look around Joe's today, there are no ordering terminals. The waiters will simply jot down on a note pad what guests want to eat and go and get it. They supervise every aspect of their orders. Only the bar and cocktail areas and the cashiers here use computers. They don't go into the kitchen, so it is their way of communicating. The waiters don't work that way."

He explained other procedures: "The kitchen here is like a ballet. Everything is laid out and choreographed so perfectly. It's amazing just to watch what goes on there."

And even carrying those heavy trays of stone crabs, each waiter must pass by a food checker on the way out of the kitchen. "It's really old school here. We have someone to do everything—check the orders, someone to do the cash payments, someone to do the credit card payments. It allows the waiters to concentrate on being the best at what they do.

"When I first came to Joe's, before the renovation and expansion, we used to be able to watch the cruise ships leave the port of Miami from my station. That was always a majestic sight. After the renovation, however, and with the tremendous growth of the high-rises everywhere, our view has vanished.

"Back in the '70s Joe's neighborhood was still an undeveloped area. There was a lot of crime all over Miami. There were no shops here. No one walked the beach. There were no cafés to have a nightcap. You'd eat and leave fast and get off the beach."

That was just forty years ago. The growth of Miami Beach has been a phenomenon that continues to accelerate unbelievably fast. And throughout the growth of Miami Beach, Joe's has been there, seen it all, and prospered.

"Take Away makes it easy for anyone to get their fix of Joe's, without waiting. You can ship signature items from our menu anywhere in the States. We've extended our hours to 11:00 p.m., and I honestly think that is because of the local teams—games get out late, and the teams and their fans head on over to Joe's post–game time."

Staying open later for dinner is also a direct result of the Hispanic influence on the community, which includes having dinner later in the evening.

The generosity of Joe's in taking care of its own comes into focus once more in Kevin's story. One summer he had emergency bypass surgery and couldn't go back on the floor. Lifting heavy trays was not allowed. "I was asked if I wanted to work at Take Away, and of course I jumped at the chance. Joe's helps its family. I had a job and I learned a lot about the other parts of our business at the same time." Another win-win.

And when Joe's waiters are out of commission, they are taken care of by their peers as well. On the black tuxedo lapels, worn by each of the wait staff, sits the coveted stone crab, a very handsome-looking, faux gold and diamond encrusted pin, which truly stands for more than just the food and service. The pin represents charity too, as all monies from the purchase of the pins, that the individual servers actually pay for themselves, are donated to charity, a different one each year. It's also used to raise money when a fellow employee is down on his luck, out sick, or for any other reason, and those tips that they rely on just aren't coming in.

It's a kind of emergency fund. And more money is raised for this fund through crab pin sales at the bars, or directly from the waiters themselves. So you can have a stone crab pin for yourself, and donate to a very good cause at the same time. And the cost is only $18!

The handsome Irishman does have a thing for some of his favorite Joe's guests. "Especially the models," he laughed. "I once gave my Joe's crab pin to Elle McPherson. She was so grateful! And Heidi Klum was here with her first husband. I loved introducing her to stone crabs" he recalled.

"You really get to know your clients," Kevin continued. "Some of our regulars know that there are things on our Take Away menu that aren't available in the dining room. Martina Navratilova was at my station one night, and she really wanted the marinated salad from Take Away. The policy here is to bring these kinds of requests to our captains, or management and I'll tell you, nine out of ten times we are always able to accommodate them!"

There are also the "unforgettable" customers.

"I know that everyone has a Jackie Gleason story here, at least those of us who had the opportunity to have known the talented performer," Kevin recalled with fondness. "He was a character. He'd sit across from the family table with his wife and would face everyone coming in. He'd be wearing a sports coast, a red carnation and handkerchief. There would always be a cigarette and a drink in his hand. And he would always, always greet everyone the same way, 'Hi ya pal!' That's one of my very favorite memories. I can still visualize his greatness today.

"We do try to establish some sort of dress code. For example, we try to eliminate the wearing of beachwear and tank tops. However there was only one person who was ever allowed in wearing a tank top. That was Hulk Hogan in his heyday. He came in his typical Hulk attire, bandana, red tank filled with holes, and he was allowed in, but just as quickly he was ushered to a corner in the Garden room."

And the joke about tank tops even got to be an ongoing gag with performer and Miamian Lenny Kravitz. "He'd wear a tank top. We'd sit him in the Garden room, and hand him a busboy jacket to cover up. He'd always come in the same way, and we'd always attempt to cover him up, the same way."

But Miami Beach is a beach town, and the ocean is less than a block away. So if you don't feel like getting out of your bathing suit, simply go next door to Take Away, or perhaps ask to be seated outside. There are ways to get your stone crabs and eat them too!

8

ANTHONY ARNESON

I have always noticed that there was something different about Anthony. Each time I came to Joe's to dine with my family, friends, or clients, he would know exactly where I had been and what new job I had gotten, and he even congratulated me when I won a coveted entertainment industry award in Los Angeles.

How did he do it? "I have a somewhat photographic memory," he explained. "I read the papers, so that I can keep up with all of the locals. It shows we care and makes each of our guests feel special." Anthony was right. It did make me feel special.

Anthony was an experienced waiter on arrival, having worked at several other Miami restaurants before coming to Joe's. Today he is a twenty-nine-year Joe's veteran.

"I actually began my career as a maître d' on the Amtrak trains, back in 1973," he pointed out. "Of course train service was quite different back then, but it did teach me a lot."

Born in Denmark, the young boy moved to the United States when he was three years old, with his father, whose specialty was building golf courses. "We settled in Spokane, Washington, where I was raised. I started traveling in my teens, and when I visited South America I fell in love with the weather. That's how I ended up in Miami. The year was 1971."

An acquaintance of Anthony's was the manager of the Crab House on 79th Street. He knew Irwin Sawitz, Jo Ann's husband at the time and father of Stephen and Jodi Sawitz. Anthony

Born in Denmark, Anthony Arneson started his hospitality career as a maître d' on Amtrak trains; he pulled into Joe's station twenty-nine years ago and has never left.

got the introduction he needed to be considered as a waiter at Joe's and landed the job. That was in 1984.

By 1987 Anthony found himself the maître d' at lunch and became a captain at night as well. I would see him in the red tie at lunch and the black tie at dinner.

"Yes, twenty-nine years is a long time, but there are lots of us who have been here that long. We started together," said Anthony. "I think the biggest change that I've seen here is the diversity of our patrons. Our clientele has become much more international.

"Of course we've grown through the years, physically. Our dining room accommodates more people. And our menu has been totally transformed. When I started here the menu and

Anthony's notes complement his keen memory for faces and help him greet return visitors by name.

the choices for our guests were basically 80 percent stone crabs. Today our food is as diversified as our guests."

Why does Anthony take the time to learn so much about his guests? "After a few years here I realized that if I'm in this business, I need to do the best I can. When someone of interest walks in, whether they are famous or one of our locals, I jot down their names on little pieces of paper."

He wasn't kidding. There are more than a hundred 4 × 4-inch bits of paper in the drawer of his podium, some faded and going back to the 1980s, all bearing names and often with a word or two beside them. One name has nothing to do with the next. The notes are not alphabetized. They are not grouped into categories. The pairings don't make sense.

"If someone walks in whom I want to remember, I write the name down," Anthony explained. "I keep the notes here at the podium. When the guest returns, even years later, if I don't remember the name when the person walks in, I smile. I never forget a face. I figure that a guest who looks familiar is someone I should remember. So I look through my notes and I always find out who it is. And then, as people are on their way out, I refer to them by name and put the name to the face. It's a great system for me and it makes our guests feel even more special.

"You know, we work for tips. Knowing who our clients are is part of what we do. I enjoy the challenge," he added.

"The Power Lunches are special. If you are here for the Power Lunch, you want to be seated on the center aisle. We call it Power Alley. We hold the aisle for our regular customers: the judges, the lawyers, the corporate giants, and the socialites. It's a great way to impress your clients, or your guests."

Was there any one moment that stood out in his long tenure at Joe's? "Absolutely, but it's not what you'd think it would be. It does have to do with a Joe's waiter though. His name was Nick. Nick Sang. Catalino Sang. He had been here at Joe's a few years, and one day he started behaving strangely. We all saw him mentally spiraling downward. It was a bit scary. Nick and his brothers owned a couple of takeout Chinese food restaurants around Miami, and apparently they owed some serious money to the IRS."

That was in November 1995. One morning everyone in the city found out that Nick had hijacked a bus, the culmination of a very stressful few weeks, and that bus had thirteen handicapped children on board. Nick threatened to blow up the driver and the kids. The heroic driver used her two-way radio, and the police were thus notified early in the saga.

Sang told the driver to take him to Joe's Stone Crab on Miami Beach, at least a forty-five-minute bus drive away. "He had been sent home early from his shift at Joe's the night before, so everyone figured there was some kind of vendetta. It was scary. And no one really knows what he would have done if he had made it into Joe's."

Police and television news crews followed the bus. They were on all sides of it, like an escort. The journey took seventy-five long minutes, and when the bus and the police got to Joe's, a SWAT team shot and killed Sang.

"We were shocked and I saw it all. It was frightening. Thank God it was early. We hadn't yet opened for lunch. There were no customers. The Metro-Dade police stormed the bus, firing the fatal shot. It was all so dramatic. I was at the front desk, and people were calling from all over. News agencies. TV stations. We were all just trying to deal with it."

Today Anthony is one of three staff members who handle the yearly Roll Call each October. Working with him on these interviews are Ed Witte and Laura Mitchell, another captain (profiled later). "I actually hired Ed, back in 1991, and now he's *my* boss. I am quite proud of that."

Anthony, one can easily tell, has a fetish for the finer things. His tuxedo shirt collars are adorned with diamond-studded accessories that were all handmade. His gold and diamond stone crab pins are *real*! His glasses are designer-expensive. This is a well-manicured maître d'—he cuts a classic figure in the role. In today's world there are only a handful of restaurants that have the position. La Tour d'Argent, one of the most expensive restaurants in Paris, overlooking the River Seine and Notre-Dame, is one of them. Commander's Palace in New Orleans is another. There are maître d's on cruise ships, and they always seem to know everything about anything, all with the utmost sophistication.

"That's their job," Anthony observed. "When you walk in, the maître d' is the first one you meet. If they know that someone famous is coming, they most likely will have done their homework in advance. The best table will be waiting."

The title comes from the French term *maître d'hôtel*, master of the hotel, or master of the house. "So basically the maître d' is the first and last to greet our guests. We know the regulars and the famous; it's the others who are an even bigger challenge. We want them to have a great time too, and a great meal and an even greater memory."

9

Jose Uchuya

Jose has been a part of Joe's extended family for twenty-eight years, but his story is one that reaches even further inside the family than most.

Originally from Lima, Peru, Jose came to Miami in 1979 with his mom and sister. He was only sixteen, and his mother wanted a better life for her children.

"None of us spoke English," Jose recounted. "My dad stayed back in Peru. He wasn't really sure that we were doing the right thing. We first lived with my mom's brother. He had seven kids; my grandparents were there too. There were about sixteen or seventeen of us all living in one house," a typical situation for migrant families at the time. "So it wasn't a surprise when after a few months we moved again, this time to New Orleans."

It wasn't long, however, before the family returned to Miami. "And that's when I got my first job in the hospitality industry, at the front desk of the Waldorf Hotel on Ocean Drive. I was working the overnight shift, and it was tough. A friend of mine suggested I go somewhere else. I did. I started working breakfasts at the Shelbourne cafeteria." This was on the beachfront, in a Miami Beach hotel. "I was a busboy and only seventeen. I wasn't happy there, since the first day my take-home was all of $1.00, and on my second day I pocketed all of $2.00. On the third day I quit.

"My next move was to a family-owned Cuban restaurant called Las Brisas de las Americas, on Lincoln Road. They hired me to make Cuban coffee. After a few days I noticed that the people who worked the stools next to me made twice what I did, so I asked to be moved to the stools. They moved me. Then I noticed that the dining room guys made even more, and I asked if I could work the dining room. I guess they liked me. They let me move up and they really trained me. I ended up as the manager there."

The young Jose was making smart moves. "I knew that if I stayed in this type of Spanish-speaking environment, however, that I'd never really speak proper English, and I'd never move into mainstream America. So my next stop was the Rusty Pelican, on Key Biscayne. I didn't have a car though, and getting there was tough."

Miami Beach was changing, and again Jose found himself relocated for the better, this time to the Hotel Carlisle, on Ocean Drive. He became a server.

At the Carlisle, Jodi Sawitz Hershey often came in to eat. "Several times, Jodi suggested that I come to Joe's, but it took a while for me to take her up on her offer.

"While I was at Las Brisas I had met my best friend George (Jorge). That was in 1979. We moved from restaurant to restaurant together and always looked out for each other. You see, George started working at Joe's before me. At that time I was at the Grand Bay, in Coconut Grove, working in a very fancy restaurant. One day I went to visit George and saw the low prices on the menu at Joe's. I asked him just how he made any money when the prices weren't anywhere near as high as they were where I was working. Of course, George let the secret out. The money was much better at Joe's. The benefits were much better at Joe's. So I went and applied. Actually I came for an interview after the yearly October Roll Call, when almost everyone else was hired that year, but even coming in late, in November, I was hired."

Arriving from Peru in 1979 and speaking no English, Jose Uchuya (*right*) worked in many restaurants before following his friend Jorge "George" Lopez (*left*) to Joe's.

Starting at lunch, Jose moved quickly into dinner. He was in the right place at the right time. "Yes," he added, "timing *is* everything." Joe's needed someone who spoke a different language to work the front door. Jose was qualified. So he became a captain at dinner, and then during the summer he served as a maître d'. That lasted three years.

"I became Take Away manager in 2000," he explained. "And that was also an invaluable experience." Jose was able to "cross train" the staff. Dining room waiters who were usually off during the summer months were able to come over to Take Away. "They made extra money. We got experienced waiters who knew Joe's inside and out. It was a win-win."

Jose's wife, Jessica, is a fifth-generation descendant of founders Joe and Jennie Weiss. Jessica and Jose's daughter Alexandria is a member of the family-owned restaurant's sixth generation.

In 2008, when Calvin Keel passed away, Jose became a dining room manager.

Jose is the second Joe's waiter I interviewed who met his wife at the establishment. As it happened, he married Jodi Hershey's daughter Jessica, a member of the fifth generation of the Joe's family, which made Jo Ann Weiss Sawitz Bass his grandmother-in-law.

"We got married back in 2000," Jose continued the story, "but I actually first met Jessica back in 1982, while I was waiting on Jo Ann and Jodi, my future mother-in-law. We would see each other over the years, and there was always a connection between us." Today Jessica and Jose are raising the sixth generation of the Joe's family, their nine-year-old daughter Alexandria.

"Jose is such a die-hard worker. He's so loyal and truly takes care of everyone in our Joe's family," said his mother-in-law Jodi.

"You know, when I came to Joe's back in '83–'84, it was special for people to go out to dinner," Jose observed. "Today you make a home-cooked meal to make people feel special. Today going out to dinner is a necessity. Think about how many meals you eat out a week, or take out. Unlike your local sushi place, or neighborhood Italian favorite, Joe's makes that time out very special."

And as far as the waiters go, "This business is for a select few. You have to love talking to people. Things you see here at Joe's, you don't see anywhere else. I look at our dining room as an extension of my dining room at home. Every night, I am the host of a big party.

"My job is about taking care of issues. I make split-second decisions. It does keep me on my toes," Jose added. "I feel that this business chooses us. It is very special."

As was the case for most of his colleagues, for Jose a major attraction to accepting a position at Joe's was the fact that he would work seven months a year, allowing five months a year for him to pursue his passion for travel. The romance with his wife took place in an exotic, faraway manner.

"We got engaged in France, on the Normandy Coast," Jose proudly told the story. "And we got married in Florence, Italy. Joe's has truly allowed me to fulfill my dreams."

10

SAMIRA (SAM) ALANI

Samira has been a Joe's waiter for eighteen seasons, having
started in 1995.

She is originally from Morocco and presently holds the dis-
tinction of being married to a Joe's waiter.

"I left Casablanca to work at Disney World, at the Morocco
Pavilion," Sam explained. Her major in college was English lit-
erature, and some of the Disney staff went to Morocco to re-
cruit people who spoke English well. "I wanted to go, and my
mom somehow put the money together to buy me a ticket. I
came to the States with $150 in my pocket. That was back in
1988, and I stayed at Disney for two years."

The young Moroccan wasn't happy living in Orlando, however, and came south to Miami at the suggestion of some good
friends.

"I got a job at the Sofitel, a French hotel in the area, and I
got to use my French. I was a server there, which gave me some
good training in the business," Sam added. "And then a friend
of mine told me that Joe's was hiring. I didn't really know what
Joe's was, but I came to Roll Call," Sam explained. "I was number 67 because I didn't arrive until about noon. Others came as
early as 6:00 a.m. Who knew that I needed to be here so early?
It was a basic interview, and then I had to pass the tray test. I
did well. Bones immediately said: 'She's in.'"

Samira Alani's fluency in several languages is an asset in providing Joe's guests the best possible welcome. Disney World first recruited her from her native Morocco to work in the United States.

Sam wasn't married when she first came to Joe's. "My husband Charaff and I were friends at the time. He didn't come to Joe's until two years after I did. He's from Morocco as well and was also an experienced waiter when he got here.

"When I got pregnant I was going to take off because I had had a previous miscarriage," Sam explained. "But Joe's management knew that I really needed to work, so they brought me into the office, which of course was not nearly as physical, and I worked as a cashier throughout my pregnancy. I answered phones at night too."

After her daughter was born, Sam returned to the dining room. "I have a chance to make people happy every day," she explained. "And I get to use my language skills too, my French, Arabic, and even a little Spanish."

Samira, with husband Charaff Gouriche—the only husband-wife pair who are both on Joe's team of waiters today.

With a twelve-year-old daughter at home today, Sam and Charaff usually work on alternate days. "And we do find time for each other. Of course, every year, we are both off during the summer. That really gives us time to be together as a family."

"There have been a lot of changes in the eighteen seasons that I've been at Joe's," Sam explained. "There's more management. Things are more organized. When I first came here, the menu was limited and we mostly sold stone crabs. Today the menu is quite diverse. I've enjoyed seeing it grow.

"Waiters don't leave Joe's without a good reason," Sam noted. "If you do leave, you either leave to start your own business, or you've won the lottery. You just don't leave here for another serving job, because no one will hire you. If you leave here, which is the best job in the industry for any waiter, there must be something wrong with you. Everyone knows you don't leave Joe's. Why would you?"

11

CHARAFF GOURICHE

"I was about to graduate from the hotel management school at home in Morocco when the king sent his minister of tourism to meet with us. His job was to pick out several students to represent the country at the Moroccan Pavilion at Disney World in Orlando. I was all of twenty-two years old and jumped at the chance, of course."

The graduating student's plans, prior to the visit from the royal representative, had been to represent his country in Germany, and so he had learned to speak German. "But the Disney team easily persuaded me," Charaff explained.

"Actually I had a choice in school. I could learn German. I could learn Spanish. Now that I'm living in Miami, I undoubtedly have chosen the wrong path!

"It was a dream for me to come to America. I was always fascinated with everything about the States. I had a two-year contract with Disney but only stayed a year, feeling there was much more I could do."

Another opportunity came to Charaff, this one with the local Miami branch of Sofitel, an upscale French hotel chain. He'd have an opportunity there to use his native French language skills.

While he was working his way up at the Sofitel, a friend sent a bright young woman for an interview. She was also from Morocco and had also just spent time representing the country at

Even though he graduated from hotel management school, was selected by Morocco's minister of tourism to work in the United States, and has worked with France's Sofitel chain, Charaff Gouriche is considered a newbie among Joe's waiters, having begun his tenure "only" in 1998.

Disney. The two quickly became friends and were friends for years. Today they are happily married, have a beautiful daughter, and are both servers at Joe's.

Charaff began serving at Joe's in 1998. It's been fifteen years, but in Joe's years he's still a "newbie."

"When I was at the Sofitel I would send many of our guests to Joe's. Everyone came back raving and everyone came back suggesting that I go work there," Charaff recalled. "Finally one day I thought I'd check it out.

"I love working at Joe's, and I love the ability I have to give my clients what they really are looking for," he added. "For example, if there is a family or a large group, I may suggest that we serve everything family style. It's the better way. Most other restaurants put everything in the same plate, the vegetables and the sauces. Here everything is served as a side, in its own dish. Customers are more comfortable this way. They can take what they want, and as much as they want.

"You know, when I was in hotel school I wanted to be a general manager in a hotel. I wanted to teach in a hotel school as well. Well, now I know that I am much better off than I was in any of my dreams. In Europe you go to school and get a diploma if you want a job in the better restaurants. In the States anyone can get a job in a restaurant. In Europe one is proud of being a waiter in a better restaurant. You work hard to get there. In the States being a waiter isn't something that one strives to be, growing up. Joe's, however, is the difference. It rivals some of the best European restaurants in quality and service. You need to come to Joe's with significant experience. Since our waiters come from around the world, some come with degrees, others with years of experience. You don't get trained here at Joe's. You bring everything you have with you. You simply learn to be better."

The husband and wife servers at Joe's don't work together. "Our stations are far apart. We hardly ever even see each other on the floor, and this formula seems to work very well," Charaff added.

"Yes, I have favorite customers—a couple from New York. They come in every year for about three dinners during the week they are in town. If I don't get them at my table, I always warn the server who does get them. Their order is not typical. They'll order a glass of wine for each of them, and they'd order two orders of Selects (that's fourteen stone crab claws, seven each). No sides. Just Selects. Then they continue to order, typically a total of eight orders of Selects at one meal. That's fifty-six claws for just two people! And then they come back the next day and do it all over again!

"But the customers who order our delicious chicken entree for $5.95 are treated the same," Charaff added. "They've all been waiting for two to three hours. They are hungry. They come to us hungry. It's a lot of pressure on us to make them feel at home right away. Within minutes of being seated they get their bread and we've taken their drink orders. And then, within another few minutes, their first course is on the table!

"I'm proud to be here. I'm proud that my wife and I can share this experience together. She can be anything she wants to be, she is so smart, but she's here for the long run. Me too. This is my last job. I wouldn't want to be anywhere else. I've learned so much from Jo Ann. She is so unique. I'd do anything for her, and I know that most of my colleagues feel the same way."

Charaff has lived in the United States for more than thirty years now, and he feels more American than Moroccan: "The culture has changed me. The cultures are so different. In Morocco, for example, only foreigners can drink in public. Muslim citizens are forbidden to buy liquor, or even to enjoy it in the privacy of their own home.

"It is always so interesting to learn the cultures and differences, what makes us the same or different," Charaff added. "Joe's affords me opportunities to meet guests from just about every country and every walk of life. I get to use my language skills a lot."

12

ANDREW RUBIN

There are not many native Floridians who work at Joe's, but Andrew certainly fits the bill.

"I started working as a busboy during school and then became a waiter at some small restaurants," Andrew explained. "But I really majored in pool halls!"

"I hadn't even heard of Joe's, but everyone kept telling me that I should work there. I had met a number of the guys during the summer and figured I should check it out."

He went to Roll Call. "I had great references from a number of people who had worked at Joe's. I made the cut. And that was thirty years ago," Andrew beamed.

As he explained it, "Timing is everything. Joe's had just expanded. I was lucky. I was given dinner shifts the year after I started, typically something that takes years. I knew that if I were working in the business, this was the place to be. I had found a home!"

Twelve years ago Andrew became a Joe's captain.

"Being a native here truly gives me an overall understanding of the many changes that have occurred over my time at Joe's," Andrew reflected. "Miami in general was a southern hick town not too long ago. But things changed with the influx of the Cubans."

In 1959, in response to Fidel Castro's new power in Cuba, many Cubans immigrated to Miami in protest. In 1980 Cuban

One of the few native Floridians on staff, Andrew Rubin has seen all sorts of changes—social, cultural, culinary, technical—during his thirty years at Joe's. But caring for the safety of employees and guests alike has always been a top priority.

refugees came in large numbers again, in what has become known as the Mariel boat lift, when more than 125,000 Cubans were illegally transported to Florida, with most of them settling in Miami-Dade County. And ever since, the Latin population from throughout South America has continued to seek out new opportunities in Miami.

"It's true. When I started at Joe's thirty years ago, there were few Spanish-speaking people working here at Joe's. Now they are the majority.

"I've also noticed the differences in our clientele over the years. When I first came here we catered to a much older group of people. They were on budgets. Today, we're seeing a more upscale group of guests every day and night. The baby boomers. They are a different class. And they have expense accounts."

Today, the captains all wear headsets to communicate throughout the three large dining rooms at Joe's. "Back when I started here, we used hand signals. Like in a football game. It was actually a lot of fun. A secret society, so to speak. It's our responsibility always to know what's going on throughout the house, and I have to admit, the headsets do make it a much more efficient process," Andrew explained as he reminisced about his time at Joe's.

"I remember, too, that thirty years ago we had cane-back chairs in the dining room. Today we have much sturdier seats for our guests. The real reason for the change: one of our heavier customers actually sat down, fell to the floor, and broke the chair in two," Andrew recounted.

"I've been a waiter at Joe's for eighteen years and a captain for twelve years. I've had the opportunity to see everybody you or I have ever heard of. And the only autograph any of us ever asked for was from astronaut James Lovell. His grandson saw that we were so impressed that *he* asked us if we'd like an autograph."

And like any good Joe's waiter would do, they asked permission. Anything out of the ordinary is always directed to the captains and the management.

"I've seen Bob Hope, Joe DiMaggio, Paul Newman," Andrew continued. "Paul was unique. He would come in and ask for a salad bowl. He likes to make his salad dressing himself. He'd tell us what ingredients he wanted, and he'd make his own dressing." Eventually, as we all know from our grocery store shelves, he began marketing his secret salad dressing formula.

"Steve Martin was funny too. As his waiter was crumbing, or cleaning his table of crumbs after his main course, Steve asked politely in a way that only would be a Steve Martin way of asking, 'Can you wrap that up for me?' He cracked us all up," said Andrew.

"I was a kid when I started. Joe's has taught me so much. Our wine list was simple back then. Today we serve some of the best wines, and we're taught about each of them so that we can share our knowledge with our guests.

"When I started here, we would see dishwashers promoted to cooks. That worked then, but today, with Chef André on board, we're also seeing culinary students come in. It's a different world today."

Over his three decades at Joe's, Andrew has seen a lot. "Our number one enemy here at Joe's is water on the floor. I remember seeing Jo Ann bending over, and on her hands and knees, mopping up the floor back when I started here. But today we have two porters whose only job is to keep the water off the floor. Every water pitcher is wrapped in cloth napkins so nothing drips. Water can be dangerous. And it is one of those safety precautions that Joe's is best at."

The safety and security of Joe's guests is a number one priority and very much a part of Joe's training. Staff are given the opportunity to learn CPR, and Joe's has its own internal Safety Committee.

There is an off-duty police officer on standby for every lunch and every dinner, and according to most of the Joe's staff, this is all part of the service, the family solidarity, created and passed down from generation to generation of the Joe's extended family.

The safety precautions set by Joe's management do save lives. I witnessed this first-hand. One night my husband and I were taking a client of ours named Steve, from Paris, for his first dinner at Joe's. As we were waiting to be seated, Steve mentioned that he needed some air. Within seconds of moving out to the courtyard, he had passed out. The off-duty officer had already called for an ambulance and within minutes I was riding to the hospital with Steve. The quick attention saved Steve's life, and before he returned to Paris several weeks later, he did get to have his first meal at Joe's.

"Joe's is so unique," Andrew concluded. "We have control of every aspect of the restaurant, from the food we serve to the welfare of our guests."

During Joe's pre-lunch or pre-dinner staff get-togethers, Andrew typically addresses his colleagues. "To the new waiters, who do typically have to wait years to become a night waiter because our turnover is so low, I tell them to be patient. To hang in there. If you wait long enough, you *will* be rewarded!"

13

MATT JOHNSON

The twenty-two-year Joe's veteran has a creative side and an ecological side that may be hidden from his guests but that are also revered by his colleagues. A native of Philadelphia, Matt is a perfect example of what waiting at Joe's is really all about.

With its seven-months-a-year employment regimen, Joe's affords every one of its wait staff the opportunity to (a) take time off over the summer, (b) indulge in a second career over the summer months, (c) work at Joe's during the two-month summer season, or (d) use creative impulses to do any of the above.

In Matt's case he actually prepares for his summertime passion throughout the year. "I collect empty bottles," Matt explained. "Beer bottles, wine bottles, liquor bottles. Did you know that over 60 percent of all waste at any restaurant is glass?

"I first spoke to Brian, our GM, about my idea, got his approval, and then went to the kitchen and to the bar and asked if I could take home the empty bottles. There's someone else here who collects corks, and someone else who collects used cooking oil.

"Yes, I'm recycling, giving these throwaway items a second life, or repurposing items that otherwise would simply be thrown away, but I'm also building up stock for my business," Matt continued.

Matt Johnson succeeded in winning one of the few much-coveted server openings through the annual Roll Call the year he applied; twenty-two years later, he still relishes the work during the busy stone crab season. He spends his time off recycling bottles from the restaurant to create tasteful home accessories.

At first he wasn't picky. He took home anything and everything that was glass. "Today, I'm more particular. I know what works best."

Along with his jewelry designer wife Naomi, he created a business. Search the web for *www.drunkenbottle.com*. They offer unique designs—lamps, candles, you name it—all produced from leftover Joe's bottles. It's a winning proposition for everyone.

Matt is a hospitality and culinary graduate from Florida International University Academy of Culinary Arts. He began his local career bartending at a neighboring beach club restaurant.

"One day someone suggested that I apply to Joe's. Since I was literally across the street, I went to the back alley and met this impressive guy, Calvin Keel, and had no idea who he was. But he did tell me to come in the next day to apply. I had no idea I'd be coming in for the restaurant's annual Roll Call, and that there would be hundreds of others applying for the same job."

Luckily for Matt, and for Joe's, he was one of six who were selected that year for the coveted positions.

"I'm sure my dad is upset that his investment in culinary school may have been money thrown down the drain, but I'm not," Matt explained. "Joe's has given me amazing opportunities. I was pretty lucky. My timing couldn't have been better, since a lot of the old-timers retired just after I started here, so I had an opportunity to move up pretty fast." Matt found the work absorbing.

"Our clientele comes to Joe's from all over the world," he explained. "With the diversity of our staff, we're able to speak with them in their own languages, and that too is important, since we all share with our guests our knowledge of Joe's, its history, the foods, the preparation, the wine, and the community. Our demographic has changed a lot too. We're seeing a much higher-end group of guests."

At the end of every season, each member of Joe's staff is given a review by management. It's a number-based review. "Mine has stayed the same for years," said Matt. "I believe in doing my job the best I can."

Unlike in other restaurants, where waiters aren't sure if their tables will be filled, waiting at Joe's pretty much guarantees all of the waiters not only that their tables will be filled but that there will be several turnovers during each shift.

"I'm sure the fact that we remain family owned and operated has something to do with that," Matt added. "Joe's is not corporate. The family goes by instinct, and their instinct has been right on for the past hundred years."

14

PAULA BERGERON

The native Miamian has been at Joe's for eighteen years. Prior to that she worked for another restaurant for nearly the same amount of time. "I guess you can say I'm a career waiter. I obviously don't like change."

Paula was working elsewhere when she first came to Joe's. "As soon as I saw the place, I fell in love. I knew I wanted to work here," she explained.

"It's been incredible. There is nothing like Joe's," Paula elaborated. "It's a special family. We're all married for seven months every year, and then we're divorced for five. That's how we all see it."

And Paula observed that it's just the opposite with her husband. "With us, we are married five months a year and pretty much divorced for seven," she laughed.

"And we do keep in touch over the summer. Especially the girls. There are about sixteen to eighteen of us now. We are all good friends."

Regarding the issue of women being a minority at Joe's: "It's not about male/female at all. It's really about who can carry the heavy, awkward trays. If you can't, then this isn't a job for you," Paula explained.

To keep in shape when she is not working over her summer vacation, Paula bikes, swims, and travels. Having just lost thirty-five pounds, she is living testimony that lifting heavy trays of stone crabs for seven months every year is the weight loss secret none of us ever knew.

"I met my husband at my last job. We were both working there, and I'd say it was love after one sautéed garlic shrimp," she laughed. "He's a great cook. I'm pretty lucky, at home and at work.

"My secret? Maybe it's being married to a younger man," she added with a wink. "And drinking only once a week. I eat well. I sleep well. I wait at Joe's. It all works!"

15

JOHN HENRY KEISER

"I remember meeting Roy when I first got here. He asked me my name. I, of course, introduced myself as John."

"We already have a John," Roy said. "So what's your middle name?"

"It's Henry. So I became Henry. But when John Dugan retired I asked Roy if I could have my name back, and that was when he began calling me John Henry, and I've been John Henry ever since."

John Henry started at Joe's in 1975. That's thirty-eight years ago. A native of Portland, Oregon, he got his server experience at the Concord, in the Catskills in upstate New York. The years were 1967–72.

"I worked weekends while I was in the service," John Henry explained. "And my dad was the maître d' in the nightclub there. One day he asked me if I wanted to go to work in Florida, because there was a strike about to take place throughout the Catskills. I jumped at the chance and came down with my friends, girlfriends. There were a bunch of us.

"I liked Florida immediately and started waiting at some of the local restaurants. I applied at Joe's twice before I got in," John Henry recalled. "I had studied hotel and restaurant management during college, and I think that helped too.

"Back in 1975 Joe's wasn't yet open for lunch. So I became a Joe's waiter at dinner. Lunch began in 1979, and I was then working two lunches and five dinners. We'd work seven months on, and we'd be off for five. So for the first few years, from 1975 until 1991, I took a summer job. I was a cab driver during my time off. I wanted the extra money.

"The food has changed through the years," John Henry pointed out. "There is so much more on the menu. The way we prepare the foods has become more diverse, more than simply grilling. The European and South American influences on Joe's and all of Miami Beach have been so great.

"I guess my very favorite guest has been Jimmy Buffett. I first heard of him when I was at a barbershop and some hippie type girl came in with his first album. I became a fan of his early on, and when he first came into Joe's and sat at my table, sometime in the 1978–79 season, I had the benefit of already knowing a lot about him. I knew the lyrics of every one of his songs, and that told me what he liked to drink—a cold draft beer—from the "Cheeseburger in Paradise" song. I was right. I brought it out for him, without him even asking. And ever since, when Jimmy Buffett comes in, he asks for me. I've seen his daughter grow up. We are truly old friends now. It's been a fun relationship.

"My brother has always been a professional poker player, and in 1991 he asked me if I wanted to go to Foxwoods in Connecticut for the summer. I had the time off. I forgot about driving a cab, so I'd work a bit there, and gamble. Great life. Eventually I gave up driving a cab in summers, but to this day, I still play poker, at least fifteen to twenty hours every week.

"I really love working here at Joe's. I get to meet forty or so new people every night and make their time with us special. It's a wonderful feeling knowing that you are able to do that for someone!"

16

JORGE "GEORGE" LOPEZ

Jorge, a Chilean native, began his career at Joe's with Philly and Anthony. That was twenty-nine years ago. The year was 1983.

"I left Chile in 1980 to pursue my master's degree in education. I was a physical education teacher back home," Jorge explained. "I had never thought of being a waiter, so my life definitely didn't go in the direction I had originally thought it would.

"I had thought I'd be attending college in the States, but there was a slight problem. I couldn't speak English. I knew I had to learn the language first."

To survive and pay his tuition, he worked in a number of restaurants. "My first job was in a Jewish hotel on 41st Street called the Crown Hotel. I was a busboy. The residents and visitors of the hotel were all older Jewish immigrants. I was a native Spanish speaker. Most of them spoke broken English with a mix of German, Russian, or Hungarian accents. I couldn't understand a word of what they said," Jorge laughed, "and they probably couldn't understand me either. And back then so many of the hotels on Miami Beach were filled with the same type of clientele—definitely not filled with the models and beautiful people you see today."

The Rusty Pelican in Miami brought Jorge his first waiting job, and he thought it would be a better way to learn English.

Follow your fate: a friendly tip about Joe's Roll Call during a red-light stop and a snap decision to abandon his master's degree brought Jorge Lopez into the Joe's family—as well as a chance meeting with the woman who became his wife.

Finding his way to Lincoln Road next—certainly not the café-lined, Victoria's Secret–Pottery Barn type of Lincoln Road we know today—Jorge credits this experience with having changed his life. "I worked at a Spanish coffee shop called Las Brisas de las Americas. I met Jose there, and he became my best friend. Jose today is married to Jo Ann's granddaughter Jessica and is the dining room manager at Joe's.

"I missed Roll Call in 1983 but was lucky enough to get an interview anyway. I knew I had to make a decision fast. Should I finish my English classes and go on and get my master's degree, or should I take the job? That was twenty-nine years ago, and I haven't regretted my decision even once," said Jorge proudly.

"Actually the story about how I got the job is quite funny. My girlfriend, who later became my wife, and I were driving along Washington Avenue. A friend of mine pulled up alongside me on his bike. It was a red light. He told me to go to Joe's because they were hiring. I didn't even know where Joe's was. And there wasn't a lot of time to get any more information than that while we were stopped at a red light. That was a Tuesday. I came in on Thursday for the interview. I saw Roy (the maître d'), and at first he thought I was here for dinner. He then gave me an application and saw that I came with the experience necessary to be given a chance. He asked me right then if I'd like to start on Saturday.

"I guess I was in the right place at the right time. I was so fortunate," Jorge added.

Joe's has been very lucky for the Chilean native's love life as well. "I had gotten divorced after eight years. I wasn't looking for anyone, but one day a very pretty, blonde all-American-looking woman came in very late in the lunch hour and sat at my table. She was eating alone. It was a Saturday. I usually didn't work during lunch, since I had already paid my dues, but fate must have truly been on my side that day. That was in the year 2000.

"It was about 2:40 p.m., and she was still there when most of the other customers had already left. I found out that she was from Texas and worked for a university there. She was here on business. Well, somehow we exchanged phone numbers. I was going to a tennis tournament the next day and she told me that she would be working. I was supposed to call her later in the day, but at that time we didn't have cell phones and the day just got away. It was after 1:00 a.m. when I finally called her. Luckily she didn't hang up on me. She told me to call her the next day, and I did, and over the next seven years we dated long distance. I would go to be with her in Texas every summer during my Joe's vacation."

In 2007 the love match became official with a huge Texas-style wedding. Jose was Jorge's best man, and a number of other Joe's waiters flew in for the festivities. Jose proudly carries those "family" photos on his cell phone today.

"Did I make the right career choice? Absolutely," Jorge affirmed.

17

OSCAR JIMENEZ

Oscar has been a Joe's employee for twenty-five years. He was one of the youngest employees ever hired.

"I grew up across the street from Joe's and had never even been inside," he recalled. "I remember seeing all of the fancy cars and pretty women walking in and out, but I never really knew what was inside. I was a big guy and at the age of fifteen, I got a job, my first job, working security for Joe's valet parking lot. As soon as I got my driver's license, I began parking cars for Joe's. We used to make $5 an hour, no tips, and that was big money for me!"

Having parked cars for two years, Oscar found his job eliminated when the restaurant changed to a more sophisticated valet system.

Oscar worked part-time as a bouncer in local clubs back then as well, and although he looks classy in his tuxedo and tie today, his air of authority still resembles that of a bouncer—a very well-groomed bouncer.

"I went to Joe's original Take Away and stayed there for two years, but it wasn't the Take Away you know today," Oscar recalled. "It was much smaller, and I used to come in early and set up all by myself. I did everything, including cooking and cracking crabs, and then I got involved with the shipping too."

At age fifteen Oscar Jimenez started working at Joe's in the parking lot, then prepped in Take Away and took a stint in Shipping before he became a waiter, exemplifying Joe's practice of mentoring eager learners and reinforcing the family philosophy.

When he graduated from high school at age seventeen, Oscar asked Calvin if he could work the floor. "Everyone said I'd make a good waiter, and I thought I would too."

To his surprise, Calvin gave the young Oscar a chance, hiring him as a busboy. "I was thrilled, because I really thought he'd only allow me to work in the kitchen. And I got to work with Bones. I loved that! I learned so much. He was a great teacher."

Oscar was a busser for four seasons, and when he turned twenty-one, he became a waiter. "That continues to be a thrill for Joe's management." Few had ever gone from being a bus-boy to being a waiter, but that started something of a trend; others would follow Oscar's path at Joe's.

"I love the Joe's family," Oscar explained. "They really care. You see, I know that first-hand. I got into a motorcycle accident during my time as a busboy. I broke both of my hands and couldn't work for two and a half months. I was going through a divorce. I had nowhere to live, and Jo Ann lent me an apartment nearby. She is amazing! And that's why we are all in love with her and with this place."

When he returned he was given light duty in the shipping department, "but I was told that when I was ready, my old job would be available. And they kept true to their word."

When he first became a waiter, Oscar worked hard. "I did seven dinners and five lunches every week. I knew I only had seven months a year to make a living, so I wanted to make as much as I could."

Today his schedule is still busy, but he finds time for his son, and his love of coaching football for inner city teams has made this part of his routine as well.

"Tipping is a funny thing," Oscar explained. "The best tippers are those who you'd least expect to be. The most generous people are those who are less demanding.

"I've learned a lot from working here," Oscar concluded. "I learned from my co-workers, guys twice my age, who are doing the same work as I do. It's hard work. You have to respect that. This is an amazing place, and I am very proud to be part of it. And you know, if I didn't work here, I'd be eating here every day. The food is that amazing!"

Joe's younger waiters, like Oscar, are very much a part of today's social media scene. Whereas many of the older waiters don't even have computers, Oscar uses one to hone his skills: "I log in and read the comments from our guests often. I like to understand what they may have liked, or didn't like, about the time they spent with us. It helps me to be a better waiter."

18

Victor Souto

Victor has been waiting at Joe's for twenty years. Originally from the warm climate of Brazil, Victor made his move to the United States in 1984, to a rather chilly San Francisco. His sojourn there was short-lived. He decided instead to study marine biology at the University of Miami.

"I started working at several local restaurants to get some extra spending money, including one at the Fontainebleau Hilton. I hadn't even heard of Joe's when I first came to Miami," Victor recalled. "It was a friend of my wife Laura who mentioned Joe's."

When Victor started at Joe's, few Brazilians frequented the restaurant—or Miami as a whole, for that matter. Things have changed a lot in the past few years. There is a tremendous influx of Brazilians, especially over the summer, and every year more choose to remain.

"This job is more physical than mental," Victor explained. "For seven months every year, it is physically demanding. I love the fact that I don't have to bring home the pressures of the office. For me, it's the perfect job. And I stay pretty fit because of it."

Like many of Joe's long-time wait staff, Victor didn't think he'd stay long. "But you get used to the pace. It's good money. Having time off to spend with the family. That's important. No other restaurant can match what Joe's has given me."

Brazilian Victor Souto didn't plan on staying at Joe's, but twenty years later, he still spends weekends with other members of Joe's extended family and jokes with regular guests, such as his "twin brother," Shaquille O'Neal.

And in his spare time? "I'm a musician. I play the mandolin. I travel. I love windsurfing. It's because of Joe's that I am able to have time to do what I love," he added.

Reflecting on the most memorable patrons at Joe's, he pinpointed two. "Rosie O'Donnell is one of my favorite guests. I always joke with her, and she always tries to imitate my accent," Victor commented. "And Shaq. He's funny. You see, I'm 5' 5" and Shaq, well, he's 7' 1". We joke together about being twins. You know, the same size. Kind of like that movie.

"This job and the Joe's family allows all of us to become good friends. I hang out with Oscar and Victor Ramon a lot. We go camping, fishing. I think the camaraderie is so important here.

"And of course I am a big Joe's fan. My family and I come here often for special occasions. It's really become home."

19

LAURA MITCHELL

When it's your turn to be seated at Joe's, there are quite a few male captains in their bright red bow ties and sharp black tuxedos who greet you warmly and show you to your seats. There is only one woman, however: a petite blonde who for the past twenty years has been waiting at Joe's.

"Each captain has his or her own dining room today. When we have tables available, we tell Ed [Witte, head maître d'] over our headsets, and by the time we get to the dining room entrance where our guests are waiting, they are ready to be seated. As I seat my guests, I ask them if they've been here before. If they tell me, for example, that they haven't been here in twenty years, I point out the old entrance and introduce them to everything new that we have added here since their last visit.

"I moved here from Long Island back in 1983. My plans were to stay a little while. Well, I'm still here," Laura divulged. "I remember visiting Miami as an eight year old. I hated the cold, even back then, and I knew that one day I'd live here."

Laura's waiting career began during her high school days, and in Miami she gained a lot of experience at some of the better local establishments. "But because of Hurricane Andrew back in 1992, I lost my job. And that's when I came to Joe's," the young mother explained. That storm was among the most

Leaving Long Island for warmer climates, Laura Mitchell got a second chance at Roll Call. Today she is not only a captain but also part of the three-person Roll Call team who conduct the annual interviews of hundreds of applicants for the most coveted jobs in the serving industry.

devastating hurricanes ever to hit Florida and many lives were changed because of it.

"I came to a mini Roll Call, I remember, but I didn't get hired the first time." That would typically take place after the regular October Roll Call. "Then, as luck would have it, in December of

'92 I got the job and started training. My actual start date was in January of 1993."

By the year 2000 Laura was offered a position as a captain and became a part of the important three-person Roll Call hiring panel, along with Ed and Anthony.

"Each of the applicants is asked the question: why should we hire you? And of course, in five minutes, they really need to sell themselves," Laura explained.

"When I started working at Joe's, Dotty Malloy, who was a waitress [and the lone female server] here for years, was a customer. Most of the managers of Joe's were women. There were four or five other women on the floor. When the whole Equal Rights thing happened, I saw women testify who didn't work here and had never even been for an interview here."

When the complaint about Joe's not hiring women as waiters came about, Laura asked the question, "How could they not notice us? What about *us*? We were women and we were waiting at Joe's. It was obvious to me, even then, that whoever was responsible for this really didn't know what they were talking about."

"We were targeted by zealots," summed up Jo Ann Weiss Sawitz Bass, "zealots only interested in hiring quotas. They didn't know the whole story."

Roll Call, according to Laura, was and still is monopolized by men applicants. "But then how many men apply to Hooters?" Laura asked. A fair question. Women and men are equal when it comes to their ability to apply for a server's position at Joe's. The tray test, however, may exclude some women and some men from passing the interview. Joe's servers do need to be physically fit.

Laura is a captain during the summer months as well. "I like what I do and I don't need time off for five months every year. I enjoy myself." Joe's wins too. They've got Laura year-round.

20

MICHAEL VAN HOOK

One of the few locals on Joe's wait staff, Michael was raised in North Miami. Ironically, he first heard about Joe's when he was working in Rhode Island over a summer break.

"I had met a couple of guys who worked at Joe's and they raved about their jobs," Michael explained. "So I came to a Roll Call, and even with the hundreds of people there for the same few open positions, I got the job. I filled out an application. Had the interview. Met with Roy and Anthony. They called me the same day. That was twenty-two years ago. It was October 17, 1991, to be exact."

From the very beginning, training is important. "You learn what could be a hazard, what should never be mixed together, how to lift properly.

"And then you add your own take. How you treat your guests. How you greet your guests. It's all part of what sets Joe's wait staff apart from all others."

As is generally the case, Michael started working lunch shifts. "It works like this: over a period of time, you lose a lunch and gain a dinner. Mostly everyone wants to work nights. There's more money. But within three years, I somehow had all nights. I was very lucky.

"A good server pays close attention to detail. You treat the customers the way you like to be treated. And I was really just a kid when I started here. I didn't know anything about wine, except that there were reds and there were whites. Today one of my passions is collecting good wines. Joe's has given me that opportunity."

New wines are introduced constantly. The vintners themselves often come in to tell the story of their wines. Education for Joe's staff is ongoing. It has to be.

Beverage Director Paul Kozolis agreed. "Our waiters need to learn what distinguishes one type of wine from another. The more knowledge, the better they will be at what they do."

Michael also has a passion for playing golf and traveling: "Joe's has taught me how to appreciate the good things in life and the good people you meet along the way.

While waiting at Joe's, Michael Van Hook has soaked up visiting vintners' training and enriched his passion for collecting wine.

Beverage Director Paul Kozolis believes the ongoing educational opportunities offered to Joe's employees are key to continuing the Joe's tradition of excellence.

"You don't have to be rich and famous to eat at Joe's," Michael made sure to point out. "We have a broad clientele. Our menu is actually quite reasonable. Everyone knows that. Yes, I've served my share of celebrities, names like Tommy Lee Jones, Owen Wilson, Willem Dafoe, and even The Situation from Jersey Shore. He actually was a nice guy. But whoever our guests are, we really do make sure they are all treated the same. The goal is to create an experience that is always unsurpassed anywhere."

21

WILLIAM JONES

The Chicago native has been at Joe's for twenty-four years now. "I started in 1989," William explained. "My father worked at Calder Race Track, and I came to Miami to live with him back in 1986. I had just finished high school. He got me a job in security at the track. I thought I wanted to be a police officer, so that was right up my alley."

While working at the track, William heard of Joe's and went for an interview. "I started sweeping floors and then became a busboy." After his third day working at Joe's, however, he tried to get his job back at Calder. "Working at Joe's was a much more demanding job!"

Calder wouldn't take him back, so he was stuck, and day by day, Joe's began to grow on the young William. He remained a busboy for about three years.

"I was a fast learner and started serving lunches after that, and I did it for ten or eleven years. I got accepted at the Miami-Dade Police Department at one point during those years, and although that was my first career choice, I really liked it here," he recalled. "So I stayed.

"Even as a busboy, I knew I was making more money than my dad did at the track. The waiters were paying 17 percent of their tips to the head busboy at that time, and he then divided the total among all the busboys. I was lovin' it.

"What happens on the floor really does emanate from all areas of the business. Chef André, for example, who has completely turned our kitchen around in the years he's been here, makes sure that the station locations are well thought out. He's made it easier for us to get in and out of the kitchen. All of that affects the way we do our job and makes us all better waiters.

"When I was a kid, every family I knew used to go out to dinner maybe once a week, or once a month, usually to the same restaurant, and it was special. Today, people dine out a lot. It's convenient, and prices run the gamut. But coming to Joe's is always special. It's where you go with your family for celebrations or with clients to close the deal. It's where famous directors learn about our community, and celebrities come to be seen in Miami. That is what always sets us apart.

"I may have been a bit youthful and militant when I first came to Joe's," William commented. "But I've learned that people are people. Joe's helped me to grow up.

"Recently I asked for some time off. I wanted to go to Pebble Beach, in California, to attend their well-known wine and food festival. Not only did I get the time off—Jo Ann paid for it! She continues to amaze me. Her generosity is tremendous. And I had such a good time. I learned so much. I couldn't wait to get back here to share everything I learned with my family at Joe's."

You can tell from William's physique that there are well-defined muscles under that tuxedo. He is athletic and swims, cycles, and runs triathlons. "Being in shape certainly helps with the physical demands of my job." During the summer months he's a personal trainer.

"All of those things, what I've become, can truly be attributed to what I've learned at Joe's. Sports had an impact on all of us too. Back when I started here, there was no Miami Heat, no Marlins. All of that too, has contributed to what has developed in our community and the type of guests we see here at Joe's.

"You know, anywhere else in the country, dining rooms are pretty much empty by 9:00 p.m. In Miami we are just getting started. We continue to be the latest night city in the country, a point that does have to do with the after-game crowd we attract today, and with the tremendous Latin influence here in South Florida as well. It's because of these two things that our dining room is packed until we close, every day."

22

KIERA HENRY.

The beautiful statuesque six-footer Kiera has been a waiter at Joe's for ten seasons. Hailing from outside Philadelphia, she first came to Miami to visit her sister Nicole Henry, who has been a well-known jazz singer in the area for years.

"I'd come down here and started working at various restaurants. I had never even heard of Joe's when I moved to Miami," Kiera recalled.

"I went to a Roll Call and passed the interview and the tray test, but I didn't pass the trailing process, so at first I wasn't hired," she explained. Trailing involves shadowing one of the full-time waiters to learn what goes into making a good Joe's server. "I didn't understand the pace. I just wasn't fast enough. That was in October of 2001."

Kiera isn't one to back down, however, and she made it a point to speak with Louis Rosales, in Human Resources. "He offered some very solid advice. He told me to take whatever job opened up. He told me to get in however I could."

In January 2002, just a few months after failing her trailing test, Kiera began working at Joe's, in Take Away.

"I was learning a lot. Jose Uchuya was the manager then and he taught me so much. My goal was to be a waiter, and to cross over from Take Away to the dining room wasn't usual," Kiera continued, "but I was in, so I had a good shot at learning the way things were."

Initially getting her foot in the door at Take Away and working hard to gain a waiter's role, Kiera Henry calls herself part of the living legacy of beloved senior manager and fifty-year Joe's veteran Calvin Keel.

Roll Call 2003 came around quickly, and this time Kiera landed the job. Another promotion from within.

"I'm quite proud of what I do here at Joe's," the outspoken and intuitive Kiera continued. "But you have to remember that nobody says they want to be a waiter when they grow up. When you become a waiter at Joe's, however, it is totally different. Totally unique. You know that unlike most restaurants, this place is here to stay. It will never close its doors. And as you know, most of Joe's waiters take that literally, because they are here to stay too."

This is the first year that Kiera and her group (the other women: Tatiana, Jeanette, and Joan) are working five nights, five dinners. "Like everyone else, we began at lunch and worked our way into nights. We're all very tight and very fortunate. Working nights is certainly where you make the money."

When Calvin Keel retired there was a celebration on his behalf. All the employees were there to honor the man who had made such a difference, for so many years.

"Calvin Keel was special. I loved him," observed Grace Weiss, the ninety-eight-year-old matron of Joe's. "At the beginning, he and I would scrub floors together. He was just a busboy then. We really and truly grew up together. He had influenced me so greatly and to this day, years after his death, his influence is still felt everywhere at Joe's."

"Yes, Calvin did a lot for Joe's, and so much for *us*, the blacks in the front of the house," Kiera explained. "All of us today, the black men and women at Joe's—who not too long ago only worked in the kitchen and had to leave the Beach at sunset—have a lot to be thankful for when it comes to Calvin. He went so far and witnessed so much, and all of the time, he carried no anger inside. He was amazing. So as a departing gift from us, we took a group photo. We told him that we are his legacy. He showed us pride, dignity, and love. He taught us so much.

"That's also what's so unusual about Joe's," Kiera continued. "This is not a corporate type of business. It is family run. There is no retirement age. In most businesses, older employees typically outlive their usefulness. Joe's doesn't get rid of its loyal staff. If they have to slow down for whatever reason, Joe's finds somewhere else where they will be useful, in positions where they can be proud and enjoy themselves.

"I believe that people in the hospitality business are smarter than other people give them credit for," Kiera concluded. "Imagine, for example, being in one position for ten, twenty, thirty plus years. You can't do that by *not* being on top of your game!"

23

MITCH ROBBINS

His nickname of "007" bespeaks both physical prowess and movie-star good looks. Indeed, Mitch of the intensely blue eyes and neatly tended hair was a skilled young tree-cutting operator before leaving the family business in New Jersey back in 1983 to embark instead on a successful career as a model.

"A friend suggested that I have some headshots made, and I started pounding the pavement in Manhattan, as they say. But every modeling agency told me that I looked too young. Then finally I landed an agent and began to model, do catalogue work, runway work, and I took acting classes."

Early in Mitch's modeling career some agents from Milan said they liked his look, and within two weeks the handsome young would-be 007 was living in Milan.

Over the next sixteen years home was in Zurich, Barcelona, Milan, and Hamburg. "Living in Europe was an amazing adventure," Mitch recalled with a wide smile that lit up those blue eyes.

"But I missed living in the States, and I ended up in Miami Beach because I figured that I could continue my modeling career here," he explained.

He spent the first seven years after his return working the night shift at the Clevelander and thus was free to book modeling jobs during the day. The Clevelander is a remodeled and now very hip bar/restaurant/hotel on Ocean Drive, in the

Mitch Robbins, nicknamed "007," is a former model and lived in European capitals for sixteen years before landing his perfect role at Joe's in 2006.

heart of what locals call South Beach. "They were wonderful people, and it was an amazing time to be on the Beach," Mitch recounted.

"I had friends who worked at Joe's, and finally in October of 2006, after hearing so much about the restaurant and its owners, I went to Roll Call. There were about 150 would-be Joe's waiters in line, all coveting the eight or so jobs that were available at the time.

"They wanted a career server. I fit the bill. I lived on the Beach. I knew the community. I was experienced. I spoke several languages." And of course he looked sharp in a tux—007 was perfect for the job. That was six seasons ago, and the rookie truly feels as though he's finally landed the perfect part.

Among 007's favorite guests were the power couple of Arnold Schwarzenegger and Maria Shriver. Perhaps Mitch felt a sense of connection because Arnold too had left his country to pursue a dream and had needed to overcome language barriers and stereotyped looks. Mitch is attracted to the power guests: President Clinton, Condoleezza Rice, and just the other day Michael Douglas came in—not a real president, but he did play one.

"When someone asks me if waiting in line at Joe's is worth the wait, I tell them it is. Go to the bar. Have a drink. Enjoy the courtyard. Have patience. It is always worth it. And you know, at the end of their meal, they always tell me I was right."

24

ROBERT BEN DAVID

It's been twenty years since the Moroccan-born Robert came to Joe's. "I was raised in the States and I used to come to Miami as a kid," Bob recalled. "My wife and I were living in Houston and we came to Miami on vacation back in 1985. Once we crossed the causeway we were hooked. We fell in love with Miami Beach. I took a job immediately."

The job he took was at an interior decorating firm, similar to a position he held in Houston. "The owner had a cash flow problem and we were doing an installation at a local hotel. I needed money since my checks were suddenly coming further and further apart, and I took a second job as a maître d' at the same hotel. Knowing what worked in the decorating business really has helped me to understand what it takes to make a good server throughout my career, there and here," Bob observed.

His career in the restaurant world had actually begun in the Catskills when he was only fifteen. He started in a catering hall, worked as a server, and then became a head waiter.

"I went to Roll Call at Joe's in October but wasn't called back until February," he remembered. "I was working locally in another restaurant when I got the call.

"Starting at lunch of course, I lucked out and kept gaining dinners added to my schedule one night at a time. By the end of my second year, I was working five nights and have been

A former interior designer, Robert Ben David enjoys the nightly stream of fashion that arrives with his guests, and he truly loves the fact that Joe's treats everyone the same, whether rich, famous, or unknown.

doing it ever since. And the new schedule allowed me time to see my kids."

What changes has he observed? "One of the biggest changes I've seen over the years among the servers is the weight," he laughed. "Not the wait, but the weight. Our weight, my own and everyone else's. We look at pictures from back then and can't believe how we've all changed. We certainly have grown up over the years, but I didn't realize until I looked at some of those photos that we've all grown *out* as well.

"Over the years that I've been part of the Joe's family there have been a number of changes of the guard. New generations. New ideas. I like the fact that no one here is afraid to try something new. Joe's has always changed with the times and I am certain that it will always continue to do so. That's so much a part of its success."

He has his own formula for success as well. "I come from the Borscht Belt, and I'm trained in what you would call tableside entertainment, having had the amazing opportunity to watch some of the best comedic talent of the day," Robert Ben David continued. "It's all about the entertainment and experience that I give my guests. Even the famous ones.

"Years ago, before he was so sick, Muhammad Ali was here. He was at my station and he asked me if I had ever knocked anyone out. I told him that I wouldn't admit it if I had, especially in front of all of his family. He laughed, and then I asked him if *he* had ever served twelve people a full order of food in twenty minutes. He laughed, shook his finger at me, and said, '*You* are the champ here, my friend.' What an amazing moment.

"And then there was the time that I had to ID the young actor Matt Damon. Boy, did I get a look! He was with a few people and picked up the tab. Well, our policy here at Joe's, if the credit card isn't signed, no matter who it is, is to ask for an ID—from everyone, even our regular clients. He looked at me funny at first, and then laughed. Just part of the routine!"

And the sense of fashion that the ex-designer brought with him? "You know, we used to decorate tract homes in Houston. We'd bring in $100,000 worth of furnishings and place them in a $60,000 tract home. But the home was still the same home. You can't change the home by putting in fancy surroundings. And it's true here as well. What you wear doesn't buy you class. You can't judge guests by what they wear. Our guests could be wearing jeans or a tux. We treat everyone the same.

"I do, however, admire fashion, and so many of our patrons are extremely fashionable. We don't have the dress code here that we had twenty years ago, but I like to see people look good. I admire our well-dressed guests and often tell them so. There are many ways to make our guests feel good. Service and good food are always first on our agenda, but compliments and knowledge of what they may be wearing actually earn points and are often unexpected, coming from the waiter.

"We have an unbelievable camaraderie among us," Bob added. "I've noticed that those who came to Joe's in the same year typically become the best of friends. Through the years they grow together. They share experiences. And because being here is a long-term commitment that we all share as well, we really do become family."

25

MOSES BATTLE

A cousin of James "Bones" Jones, Moses has been in the Joe's family for thirty-six years, a few years less than his cousin.

"I started here in 1977," Moses recalled. He came from Georgia, got out of the service in 1976, and headed for Miami to have fun. His sister was already living in the city, and his cousin was already a Joe's employee. "I started in the kitchen, where my brother had worked, and I was washing dishes. It was a very old dishwashing machine."

Calvin Keel was the manager, and as was so often his way when he spotted capability, he asked whether the young newcomer wanted to be a busboy. "I had a week to learn and was a busboy from that first year until 1993." Then Moses asked Jo Ann if he could be a waiter, and he's been enjoying waiting at Joe's ever since.

"If you were black back then, you needed to carry a 'Beach Card', an ID that said where you worked and who you worked for. You had to leave Miami Beach by midnight, but I didn't mind. I had more fun on the other side. There was so much going on after hours." The jitneys were gone by then, and he could drive over the bay from Miami to Miami Beach, but the after-midnight curfew for blacks remained.

He had served his country. He had fought for freedom and rights for everyone. "And I still needed that card to cross the bay! It is what it is. It was what it was." But it's all over now; the

After serving his country in the U.S. military, Moses Battle joined his cousin Bones at Joe's in 1977; Calvin Keel plucked him from the dishwashing staff to join the bussers, and Moses worked from there to earn his promotion to waiter in 1993.

curfew ended in the late 1970s, soon after Moses started work in Miami Beach.

"And the area around Joe's has changed so much too," he added. "There were all elderly people in Miami Beach when I first came here. It was basically a place to come to retire. There was little restaurant competition.

"Calvin taught me to work hard. He shared his tremendous work ethic. I still come in, even when I'm sick. He was a great influence on all of us. He was the one who led the way and set the standard," Moses recalled with much fondness.

"Jesse Weiss was a great teacher too," he added. "I remember one day when he cursed me out for something. I'm not sure why he did that, but the next day he gave me $10 and asked if I was all right. I liked him.

"Yes, I have my regulars, but I like to treat all of my customers like they are rock stars, no matter who they are. I treat them all the same."

26

GREGORY ZAFF

Greg is a second-generation Joe's employee. His father, Leo, worked as a waiter at Joe's in 1937–38, and Greg used to play with Jo Ann when she was a little girl, in the alley behind the kitchen.

Greg has been at Joe's thirty-five years now. "I came to Miami by boat. It took two and a half months," he recalled. But the boat he was traveling in was not coming from Cuba or some other exotic destination. Greg was coming from Brooklyn.

"It was my boat, and a friend and I decided to take our time," he reminisced. "I knew once I got to Miami, I'd have to get a job, so I took my time.

"My dad trained me to be a waiter in New York and got me my first job there, as a busboy, where he then worked as a server. On my first day I served ice water to a woman who was wearing a very, very low-cut blouse. Well, I guess I was looking a little too much, when I happened to pour the water down the front of her shirt. That was bad enough. But when I bent over to help, I tore the seat of my pants! Of course, I immediately told my dad that I didn't think this business was for me. But he tied an apron around me and said to go on like nothing ever happened, and I did!

"Dad didn't think it was a bad start, and he encouraged me

to keep trying. We even worked together for a while," Greg remembered warmly.

"In 1978, after I first came to Miami, a friend of mine told me that Joe's was hiring waiters. One of my pals told [maître d'] Roy and the Weisses about me, and I got in. It was during mid-season, and there was a need for experienced waiters," Greg noted.

Once he started, he didn't stop. He worked thirty-five consecutive days: "I wanted to prove myself." And thirty-four seasons later, he's still there.

"Every day is a good day. Some better than others. But there are no bad days at Joe's," Greg smiled.

Greg has had the honor of becoming what is known as the "assistant family waiter," an esteemed position within the ranks of Joe's waiters. He would be a waiter for the family, for Mr. and Mrs. Jesse Weiss, twice a week. "They would have dinner in the dining room, at the family table, usually at about 4:30. The table was positioned where they could see everything that was going on anywhere in the dining room (it was before our current renovation, where we have separate dining areas). If they were having guests, they'd sit down to eat later in the evening. And the Weisses knew everyone. Even Elizabeth Taylor."

Jackie Gleason would sit opposite the family table. "He'd come in early and smoke a cigarette and drink Crown Royal Manhattans, maybe three or four," Greg added. "And he was a very generous man."

He was not the only one. "I had one regular client who would come in every week. That man was such a generous tipper. He didn't know it, but he was actually paying my mortgage with those generous tips, for fifteen years!" Now that could only be a waiting at Joe's story.

"When I started working here, the area was a slum. The Miami Beach Kennel Club was across the street, and that's about it," Greg observed. "It was a wasteland. And over the years things have changed. Joe's is bigger. The menu is bigger. The area is filled with luxury million-dollar high-rise condos and expensive eating establishments."

The shifts suited him well. "I am a professional waiter. My father trained me. I take pride in what I do," Greg added. "We all do. That is what makes us Joe's caliber!"

Greg is also proud to be in charge of the Waiters Fund, where, as mentioned, proceeds from the sales of the faux gold and diamond stone crab pins go to helping the Joe's family when needed. "We give to other charities too, all coming from the money we raise by selling the pin, but our first priority is always our brothers and sisters."

The proceeds from pin sales also are used for taking care of the kitchen staff and cashiers at Christmas. "It is our way of giving back and saying thanks," Greg commented. "They are all a very important part of what makes us good at what we do."

Although waiting at Joe's is physically and mentally demanding, after hours Greg would work a second job, as a painting contractor. And since Joe's was open only seven months out of the year for most of Greg's career, he would then take the time to rest over the summer. "I'd go to the track at Saratoga and bet on every race. But I'd always get back to Joe's in time to paint the dining room before the season would begin," he laughed. "I really enjoyed that!"

27

Jaime Lagunas

The Chilean native left his country and moved to Europe, and then to Toronto, where he got married. "But the Canadian weather wasn't making us happy," Jaime recalled. "So we decided to move to Miami."

Jaime began his waiting career at a famous restaurant in Toronto and first came to Miami on vacation. He was a Joe's customer the first time he stepped up to the podium.

He moved south in 1971 and worked at a number of well-known area restaurants during his first fifteen years in what he calls the tropical heaven. "And then a friend told me that there was an opening at Joe's, and I went to Roll Call. I remember that Stephen's father, Irwin, was here, and he knew I had worked at some of the best places in the city. That helped me to get the job.

"As soon as our guests are seated, I always introduce myself, and I ask if they are familiar with our menu, or if they've never been here before, I tell them about Joe's and our signature dishes," Jaime explained.

"I'm proud to sell our food. I'm proud to work for such a good family, in one of the very best restaurants in the United States. Joe's allows me to be the best I can be at what I do."

And Jaime's best happens to top everyone else's, at least in two respects. Number one: Jaime has won just about every

Jaime Lagunas first came to Joe's as a customer, and now the Brazilian native leads the green team—recycling green team, that is—collecting about twenty gallons of used cooking oil from the restaurant each week to power his beloved biodiesel automobile.

internal contest Joe's has held. Competition is always fun and typically keeps people on their toes, and Jaime is good at it.

Joe's very first internal contest for the wait staff was a wine competition. The waiter who sold the most bottles of Glen Ellen wine in a single season would win a trip to the winery, located in the beautiful wine country of Sonoma, California. Sure enough, Jaime won. He and his wife and son made the trip, with VIP treatment throughout. "I was treated as if I were a real celebrity. It was amazing."

The following year Jaime won another wine contest, this time for selling the most B.R. Cohn wine, and again he found himself living a dream among some of the world's finest grapes. There have been other prizes too; Jaime has won turkeys, more wine, and even meals prepared by Chef André.

"I am a good salesman, and actually that is one of the skills I picked up living in Spain. I sold books there when I was younger, and I did well. Everything I learned way back then has been carried with me all these years, and the same rules apply here at Joe's. A good salesperson is a good salesperson, period."

And there's a second area in which the winningest Joe's waiter excels. Number two in what sets Jaime apart from his colleagues lies in being green. It surprised me as an attribute for a waiter, but it's true.

Jaime drives an older Mercedes, a 1987 diesel model called the 300SDL. Gas became expensive several years ago, and Jaime heard of a chef using vegetable oil to make biodiesel for running the car. He moved quickly on the concept.

He asked permission in the kitchen and began collecting about twenty gallons of used vegetable oil every week. It takes about two to three days to make the solution, but the car has nearly 210,000 miles on it, and continues to run like a baby. Who would have thought a busy waiter at Joe's would also be a leader in keeping green?

"I never go to a gas station," Jaime concluded. "And there is no pollution. I love my car, and I'm proud of this discovery and my ability to reuse the oil. That's a win-win for Joe's and for me!"

28

Niksa Rakic

A twenty-five-year veteran of the waiting game, Niksa is a Croatian native who went to hospitality school back home and began his service career on cruise ships. As luck would have it, on a cruise was where he met Roy Garret, who at the time was Joe's head maître d'.

"I hadn't even heard of Joe's when I arrived in Florida. My fiancé was a Miami native, who told me she knew of the place and that I'd have to wait in a long line to get in because it was always so busy.

"Well, I guess I really impressed her the first time we went to Joe's, because as soon as Roy saw me, he gave me a big smile and a hug, addressed me by name, and ushered us right in! It was the first time I ever tasted stone crabs."

The first time Niksa went to Roll Call, in 1999, he was not accepted. There were only a few positions open. He wasn't discouraged, however, and in 2001 he made the cut. He started as a lunch waiter.

Twelve years later he approaches his job "as if it were my own little restaurant. I'm in charge of making sure my guests have a great time. It's very old school, very detailed, and I am very proud of what I am able to do here at Joe's. I am here for the long run."

Working on the cruise ships was an adventure, but Niksa also found it limiting: "I never had the interaction with my

Undeterred by a first rejection at Roll Call, Niksa Rakic landed a spot at Joe's in 2001 and has fallen in love with the extended family, the details of the job, and the always-changing interactions with guests.

guests the way I do here at Joe's. That's one of the reasons I love it here!"

Niksa maintains a demanding pace, working five nights a week and two lunches. Wearing a red bow tie at lunch, Niksa is a captain. At night he sports a black tie and serves his guests.

"Tom Cruise was at my station, and yes, he ordered stone crabs. I found him to be very humble, and he was a generous tipper."

Niksa knows that a Joe's waiter must always be ready for anything. "I've had red wine spilled on my white shirt, and of course there is always an extra shirt in my car. A Joe's waiter is always a step ahead."

Croatia is beautiful, according to Niksa, but so very different from Miami—the winters are cold and snowy. "Sunny Miami is home now. I love it here and I love to run and fish and spend time with my family. Both families, because the Joe's family is now my family too."

29

JEFF REYNOLDS

He's not a waiter, but he does find himself waiting at Joe's. Jeff became a bartender at Joe's twenty-eight years ago. The native of Newport, Rhode Island, felt a part of the Joe's family immediately.

"For someone to get a job at Joe's as a bartender, one of the existing bartenders has to die or retire. Joe's employees basically fire themselves. That's how it works here," Jeff explained.

"I get to speak with our guests while they are waiting to be seated," Jeff continued. "With our most recent renovation, we've opened up an entire new section for our guests with bar stools, booths, tables, and plenty of room to hang out where it's comfortable and pretty, and we offer bar food too, if the customers are interested."

He acknowledged: "Sure, they may get tired of waiting. But it's never a surprise that they have to wait. When guests come to Joe's, they know there are no reservations taken and it's first come, first served. I help them get through that part. Often I'll tell a joke, a Joe's story, share some of our history, or do a bit of magic for them. We're all part of the bigger picture here."

Twenty-eight years ago there were perhaps four choices of red wine, perhaps a few more of white. "Today our wine list includes hundreds of labels, of all price points. Jo Ann, like her father before her, always insists that our guests should be

Jeff Reynolds has tended bar at Joe's for twenty-eight years, and he appreciates how certain things—the wine list, the barware—always change with the times, but the important things—taking care of Joe's family and guests—never do.

able to afford Joe's. The food or the wine. There's something for everyone here.

"The tastes of our guests certainly have changed through the years, too. When I first started at Joe's we kept our recipes simple. There were no blended drinks. No mojitos. We're seeing more requests for martinis today, and in recent years have changed our old Joe's signature martini glass for a more traditional type martini glass. Like anything else, things must change," he added.

"When I first came to Joe's, I told my mom that all the waiters were old. They all had gray hair. Well, now I have gray hair too. It's been nearly thirty years, and Joe's has given me so many opportunities. I've grown older and wiser. And I've had chances to pursue my passions, such as my ability to work with kids with disabilities, helping them to enjoy life. That's what it's all about. We all have such unique and diverse interests here at Joe's, and we're all encouraged to maintain those interests."

And when needed, as we've heard so many times before, Jo Ann has often come to the rescue of her extended family.

"Jo Ann and her family have put hundreds of kids through college. They've afforded so many of their staff chances to buy homes. That's what has been created. But Jo Ann looks out for us in other ways too. One day, for example, I bought some bicycles for some disabled kids. I was driving down I-95 and there was traffic. I was late for work. I hit a bump, and wouldn't you know it, the bikes went tumbling off the roof of my car and directly into traffic. By the time I turned around and came back to pick up the bikes, they were gone.

"I called the restaurant and told them I'd be late. Jo Ann asked me why, because I think she sensed a bit of panic in my voice. I told her the story, and when I got to work, she asked me how much the bikes were and gave me a check on the spot to replace them. That's the kind of person she is. And that's the type of lessons we've all learned here at Joe's."

30

STEVE HAAS

It's been thirty-two years since Steve Haas was seen waiting at Joe's. Steve is now the proprietor of one of Miami's most popular new restaurants, City Hall, just across the bay from Miami Beach and Joe's.

"I like to ask, 'When did Joe's become Joe's?' I mean when did Joe's really and truly become a household name? If you conjure up names like Sinatra, J. Edgar Hoover, Clark Gable, Bing Crosby, JFK, Jackie Gleason, and the like, you'd have to say the '60s. To me, that's when Joe's became Joe's as we think of it today," Steve Haas commented.

He grew up in Miami Beach and spent a lot of his youth working in his parents' coffee shop and deli. "It was the Normandy Coffee Shop and Sam's Deli," Steve explained. "Meyer Lansky [the mobster] would come into that deli every day."

Steve majored in marketing and accounting at nearby colleges and proudly declared that he has never lived anywhere but Miami. Perhaps that's why he chairs the Greater Miami Convention and Visitors' Bureau today.

He tried to make it at a conventional desk job, but it wasn't for him. "My first real waiting job was at the 94th Aero Squadron near the Miami International Airport."

In 1979 Steve found himself working at the prestigious 41 Club, next to The Forge. "The Forge wasn't hiring, so I somehow manipulated my way into the $5,000-a-year membership-only

Steve Haas stopped waiting at Joe's to start his own restaurant, taking with him key lessons taught to him by Jo Ann Weiss Sawitz Bass—namely, embrace your customers, and never expect your staff to do something you aren't willing to do yourself.

private club," Steve explained, "and stayed until it closed a year later."

Steve ended up next door, at The Forge, and was made head maître d', catering manager, and restaurant manager, all by the age of twenty-three.

"I knew I loved this business, so I was ready for anything that came my way," he added.

By 1980, when Steve was working at The Forge for dinners, he heard that Joe's was opening for lunch for the very first time, and he went to Roll Call to apply for a position. He got it and worked lunches five days a week for two years at Joe's, plus dinners at The Forge.

As exciting as the 41 Club was, nothing can be compared to Joe's, according to Steve Haas. "The family is always on the floor. They are always involved. Even Jesse Weiss. And he ran the place with such intimidation. It was easier for the waiters back then because 90 percent of everything Joe's had on its menu was served cold. But their systems were strenuous, even then. They have a unique checkout system that the waiters need to pass before they deliver any order to their tables. You have to get it right!

"I can tell you," Steve Haas admitted, "back when I started at Joe's, it was largely a homophobic world. No one talked about being gay or not gay. Some of the waiters who knew I was gay said I should keep quiet. It was a subject that simply wasn't discussed at Joe's, or anywhere at the time," although according to Jo Ann and Stephen, it wouldn't have mattered a bit. "It was just how things were in society back then. There were, however, a few other waiters who were gay too, so I was able to discuss my thoughts and opinions with them.

"And when it came out, it really was never an issue, not for anyone. Jo Ann and I were then, and are today, very good friends. She is, in fact, one of my very favorite people of all time. I like to think that I run my restaurant today like she runs hers. Jo Ann, on any day, would be cleaning the floor, clearing tables, bussing tables. She would never ask anyone to do anything she wouldn't do herself.

"Since I was at Joe's only a couple of years, because everything I did at The Forge was so demanding, I jumped at the chance of replacing Roy, the head maître d' at Joe's, when I heard he was retiring about six years after I left," Steve recalled.

Steve asked his friend Jo Ann for the job, but there was a slight problem. Steve wasn't working at Joe's, and to become a maître d', you needed to be promoted from within.

"Joe's and The Forge were my college, my university," Steve explained. "I worked seven days a week and didn't mind. I lived large. I spent large. And I had a ball."

On reflection, said Steve, "The most important thing that Jo Ann taught me was to respect my employees. That I needed to do anything that needed to be done, even as an owner. She taught me that no one is ever above you, or below you. You are always a team!"

His tribute to Jo Ann Weiss Sawitz Bass and Joe's continued: "Jo Ann taught me that there is no ego in this business. That you need to remain humble and as down to earth as you can. In all the years I've known Jo Ann, I've never heard one negative word about her.

"My favorite Joe's story: That's easy! Joe's used to seat patrons until 10:00 p.m. At 10:00 p.m. sharp the light at the maitre d' podium would go out. That was the staff's cue, warning them that no one else could be seated and that the kitchen was closed. Well, as a waiter, you never wanted to get the last table to be seated. Ever! You see, Jesse Weiss lived above the dining room, and he would never go upstairs until the last guest left. He would wait around, and he'd press the waiters to get late customers out, no matter who they were.

"One night I did have the last table. The guest was a single man. I was rushing. He was sitting and eating and reading his newspaper—slowly. The only person left in the large dining room, and he was *reading the newspaper*. Finally Jesse came over and said: 'What do you think this is, a library?'" The startled customer paid and left." Delicacy was not Jesse's greatest attribute.

"After hours everyone from Joe's and The Forge would hang out at the Irish Pub, on Miami Beach. It was part of our culture in those days. We all really enjoyed one another. I worked with Philly and Bones, Andrew and Jose, Anthony and Brian, Nate and John Henry. We have great shared memories, and many of them come into my own establishment today."

When Steve created the restaurant City Hall, he needed a name that would tie his two lives together: restaurants and civic politics. "It was perfect," he added.

"I believe I've been able to bring everything that Jo Ann and Joe's taught me to my own restaurant," Steve concluded.

"I embrace my customers. I respect my staff. I do whatever it takes. Jo Ann taught me, and all of us, that it is all about service and commitment. Joe's is and will always be my favorite restaurant because of what's inside.

"Why is Joe's still around today?" Steve asked. He answered his own question: "It's because like anything else with longevity, a restaurant too has to evolve. The world was, of course, dramatically different a hundred years ago. What wasn't? But through the years, Joe's has changed, adjusted, and stayed ahead of everyone else.

"Happy Birthday! I wish Joe's and the Joe's family everything they wish for themselves and more. No one deserves it more, and no one has earned it more."

III

THE WAITERS' SUPPORT

31

ROSE McDANIEL

She is not a server at Joe's. Never has been. But Rose McDaniel has been at Joe's on and off over the past fifty years. She is best friends with Jo Ann Weiss Sawitz Bass. "And I'm sure the reason Jo Ann first asked me to come to Joe's to work is that she felt sorry for me," Rose explained.

"We didn't know each other, but Jo Ann and I had a mutual friend, and we found ourselves at the same dinner party," Rose recalled fondly. "When she met me, Jo Ann told me I looked like the '50s movie actress Jan Sterling. I told Jo Ann I didn't like Jan Sterling, 'so I'm not so sure I'm going to like you!'"

The exchange opened up the doors, and the two became fast friends. That was fifty-six years ago.

"I was divorced, and Jo Ann was afraid I didn't have enough money. She'd come to visit me in Hollywood (Florida), where I lived, and she'd put food in my refrigerator. One day she said, 'Why don't you come in to help mother at night and be a cashier?' I told her that it sounded as if it could be fun, and before I knew it, I became a fixture at Joe's."

Today Rose McDaniel oversees everything that goes on in the dining room during the lunch hour. "I'm a real stickler for cleanliness, that's my big thing," she added. "But what keeps me here and in love with what I do is the Joe's family. There is no way to explain the closeness we all have. I loved Jo Ann's father, Jesse. He was the type of guy who really would give

Since meeting Jo Ann Weiss Sawitz Bass fifty-six years ago, Rose McDaniel has had a long understanding of and true appreciation for the generosity and friendships in the immediate and extended family at Joe's.

you the shirt off his back, and he had an amazing sense of humor.

"One day there was a bird in the restaurant, and someone asked Jesse Weiss the obvious: 'How did a bird get in the restaurant, Jesse?' He shot right back with, 'Isn't that obvious? He tipped Roy $20, of course!'"

"And I love Jo Ann's mother Grace," Rose added. "We're good friends till this day, and we even travel together."

Grace Weiss explained: "Jesse and I both loved Vegas, and we've been going there since 1942, when Bugsy Siegel was beginning to plan his grandiose gambling community. I still go to Vegas. Rose McDaniel and I often go together. We have so much fun. You see, friendships that are made at Joe's truly do last a lifetime."

According to Rose, it is really difficult to find anything wrong with anyone at Joe's. She summed things up this way: "The staff all want us to succeed, and they all do the best they can, always."

32

DOTTY MALLOY

Dotty Malloy waited at Joe's for seventeen years. For the majority of her service she was the only female on the wait staff. "Dotty was still waiting at Joe's when I started on the floor," Steve Haas recounted. "What a character she was!"

"Dotty became a customer after she retired," remembered Laura Mitchell, Joe's only female captain today. "It was a bit intimidating if you had Dotty at your station."

As waiter Kevin Murphy explained (see part II), Dotty called him her nephew and appointed herself to smooth his way— "She taught me so much!" said Kevin.

She was bigger than most men, according to the combined recollections of the group. She wouldn't let them get away with anything. She hung out with the guys. The only difference? She didn't have to wear a tux. She would come in every day wearing her own uniform, a black jumper and a white blouse. Today the women do wear tuxedos.

"I agree," Paul Kozolis added. "Dotty was a tough, hard, Irish woman from Boston. Hard as nails! She wouldn't take strife from anyone. She had a personality like a man. Her husband Johnny worked in a local bar. They had similar strong personalities."

33

BRIAN JOHNSON

In the opening pages of this book we met the former waiter [MAD] Brian Johnson, now general manager for Joe's. He has been in the restaurant business since he was eleven years old.

"And at sixteen I had an argument with my parents and left. I ended up renting an apartment on my own in Jamaica, Queens—the only white kid in an all-black neighborhood. I worked two jobs to make it, and went to school too."

Over the years Brian was a waiter, bellhop, server, sous chef, broiler cook, and manager. He worked at Gurney's Inn in Montauk, Long Island; worked throughout the Catskills; was a bartender; rose into management; and was once proclaimed a saucier, king of sauces, by a chef with whom he apprenticed on Long Island. Every step he made brought the self-proclaimed restaurant professional more knowledge.

"But the chef who made me a saucier was also the one who told me point blank, 'Get out of the kitchen.'"

After a number of years learning the business, Brian found himself in Amherst, Massachusetts, enrolled in a hotel program. There were a lot of miles between school and his part-time job, and one gusty, snowy day, facing a near-death drive to work, he decided that the image of his friends in Miami—going to the School of Hospitality at Florida International University and studying by the pool—looked very tempting. Brian

General Manager Brian Johnson has held a dizzying range of positions in hospitality—from bellhop to server to saucier to Joe's waiter—and draws on all of it to meet both everyday and unexpected situations.

fled to Miami, graduated from FIU, and then took a job at the Sheraton Center back up north in New York City.

"One late night I went to get my car in the employee garage. My car, with me in it, got stuck in the elevator in the garage. No one was around. There was nothing I could do. There were no cell phones back then. I spent the night in the car. Guess that was a sign," Brian decided.

"So I headed right back to Miami. My first job back here was at Cye's Rivergate. Cye fired me at least five times, but I never got out of the door. Apparently he fired everyone the same way.

"One day I came to lunch at Joe's. A friend of mine from Gurney's was working here. His name was "Fast Eddie" Rolle. That was in November of 1980. Eddie suggested I come here and work as a waiter. He knew I had the experience. Of course, he told me to speak with Roy. Well, luck was finally on my side. Even though Roll Call for the year had come and gone, Roy told me to trail [follow another server] the very next day. I jumped, handed in my keys to Cye, and became a part of the Joe's family right then."

As he describes himself, Brian is a facilitator. "That's what I do best. I make things happen." The GM also refers to himself as the chief cook and bottle washer, trouble-shooting everything that goes on in the front of the house, and in the back of the house—the kitchen, Take Away, and Shipping, and even with the valet service. He certainly has the experience in the industry to confront any problem or situation.

"Being a waiter at Joe's is a different experience today," Brian added. "So different than when I started. I remember when I first came here I had to be fingerprinted and get a police ID just to be allowed to go to work on the Beach. At that time, everyone had to be fingerprinted in order to get a job on Miami Beach."

He likes the fact that Joe's has always evolved with the times. "I like to believe that I'm helping to steer Joe's into the future," Brian added. "We're always thinking ahead. That's really the secret of our success."

Yet he also makes sure that the staff retains Joe's traditions: the finger bowls, for example. That's been a Joe's tradition for many years; no one can quite determine how many. "When we had a water shortage a few years ago, we tried other things—wrapped wet napkins, hand towels—but we went back to tradition. The silver finger bowls, served at the end of the meal, are part of the Joe's experience. And honestly, I can't remember another eating establishment anywhere in recent years where they serve finger bowls. Yes," confirmed COO Stephen Sawitz, "Our finger bowls, like our bibs, are here to stay."

"And yes," Brian added, "now and then a customer will sip the water in the finger bowl, or even eat the lemon slices floating on top, a sight that does make all of us laugh."

34

CHEF ANDRÉ BIENVENU

I hadn't intended to interview Joe's executive chef as part of the story of waiting at Joe's, but for Joe's waiters today, it seems, all roads lead back to the incredible Chef André who joined the team fifteen seasons ago.

It is true that Joe's waiters—all of them, the older and more experienced as well as the newbies—credit Chef André with making their jobs run more efficiently and smoothly. Nearly all the long-time waiters describe their time waiting at Joe's in terms revealing that the situation before and then after the André influence has been like the difference between night and day.

Chef André had plenty of experience before coming to Joe's, but it was in the corporate world, where he worked for the Hyatt organization for many years.

"Just about every one and a half years or so, I'd be transferred to another city. My wife certainly wasn't happy about another move, and my kids were at an age when it really mattered," Chef André explained. "One day a head hunter called me. Apparently Joe's was looking for a change. They needed an executive chef. They had never had one before.

"I was used to the corporate world. I wasn't sure what to expect. So I came down to Joe's all prepared to meet with the people in charge of hiring, and Stephen Sawitz walked in, fresh from his morning run. He had shorts on. He was wearing a

Chef André Bienvenu has elevated the culinary experience and perfected the kitchen's organization since arriving at Joe's fifteen years ago.

fanny pack. He was sweating. Not quite what I expected," Chef André laughed in recalling his first look at his new boss and at Joe's.

Up until this point, the menus at Joe's had always been family run. The recipes were all on handwritten index cards in Jo Ann's office. Most of the kitchen staff had been at Joe's so long that they had those recipes memorized. "My first dinner at Joe's, my wife and I had steak and fish, and I didn't think it was that good. I wasn't impressed. But I did like Stephen. I liked his direction. We talked a lot. I knew that this would be a challenge, and one that I was up for, so I took the job," the chef recounted.

"My first couple of years here, I listened. I observed. I learned a lot from our employees. That was my goal. For the first two years that I was here, I didn't touch the food. I knew I had to learn before I could implement changes. And at that point, I'd say that 95 percent of our sales were stone crabs."

While continuously expanding and refining the menu selections, Chef André and his staff know that the stone crab will always remain the star attraction.

Joe's number one asset is employees, whether front of the house, back of the house, in the kitchen, or somewhere between the two realms, like the bussers pictured here.

Procedures may have changed in recent years, but recipes for classics like the homemade chips have not.

Joe's is now known for near perfect steak and fish dinners, and those sales now almost match the sales of the signature stone crab on a daily basis.

The staples are the staples at Joe's. The recipes haven't changed through the past hundred years, but Chef André has changed the way they are prepared. The spinach, for example, is now much greener. It looks more appetizing. But the taste is the same. "The procedures needed to be updated. We did that. But I wouldn't dare change the recipes." Thus the influence of Joe's early days is still reflected on the menu. Joe's keeps its recipes intact, with just a bit of updating through the years.

Chef André focused on serving procedures as well. "Our biggest asset at Joe's is our employees. That's the reason for our success. It's also the way the family treats its employees, its customers, and the community. I've never seen anything like it," the chef added. "The family, the Joe's family, is so generous, and they want nothing in return. That's just the way they are.

"I wanted to make it easier for the servers. I knew right away that this was what mattered most. They are my salespeople. They are my public relations team. If there were difficulties in their doing their job, I wanted to focus on eliminating those difficulties. That's where I started to make my changes."

Chef André runs a calm kitchen. No yelling. No tantrums. "I want my salespeople, the wait staff, to feel calm, and that has to start with me and my kitchen."

Because of Chef André the kitchen at Joe's today runs like clockwork. And the first course really does come to the table in minutes. "Our servers are used to speed. Our seats turn over a lot, and that is truly because of our ability to serve quality food, fast. When people come here, they are hungry. They've waited a while to be seated. We want them to remain calm too."

Chef André has made it easier for the waiters to pick up their orders—to get in and out. He knew that would be one of the most important changes he could implement at Joe's.

The lunch and the dinner menus today are different too. So is the summer menu. "We don't change a lot, but in the summer, when we don't have fresh stone crabs on the menu, we can be more creative with our fish and meats and even the sides. There's also a large Brazilian influence that you'll find in our menu over the summer."

After the Mariel boat lift came to Miami more than thirty years ago, Hispanics became a majority in the kitchen at Joe's for the first time, replacing the great southern black influence that had played a primary part in Joe's kitchen for so many years. The black kitchen staff, in turn, were promoted and became bussers, and one was promoted to become Joe's first black waiter.

"Our lunches are known as Power Lunches. It's a who's who of the city, and we do cater to their needs as well. The lunch crowd is typically older. The dinner crowd is younger, and there are more families," added Chef André.

He swore he wouldn't stay at Joe's over a year, according

Knowing that the kitchen environment makes or breaks the dining experience, Chef André re-engineered the system so that waiters could pick up their orders efficiently, quickly, and calmly.

to Jo Ann. "He's now in his fifteenth season, and two of his children have worked in his kitchen," she noted. "André knows each one of his staff personally. He really cares. If they are good and show an interest, he'll invest in their future and send them to Le Cordon Bleu, the prestigious cooking school. He is truly amazing!"

Chef André has about a hundred people on his staff, including two executive sous chefs, whom he refers to as his right hands. "Their job is to make certain all of the employees are at their best. They are my eyes," he said.

About forty-five members of the chef's staff are still there from when he started fifteen years ago. "I think the biggest kick I've had is watching their loyalty to me grow. I knew I had to prove myself, and watching that happen has been the biggest success in what I could ever hope to achieve."

As Jo Ann observed, the chef knows everyone on his team personally, from the dishwashers to the first cook. He knows their children's names, their grandchildren's. "They are all here for the same reason: to take care of their families. And if I can make their work time happier and easier and better, that's what I want to do. Many of the staff happen to be related, and we welcome that. An ethic of hard work is difficult to find, and when it runs in families, it makes it even more special," Chef André commented.

"I want our guests to say they have just had the best fish, the best steak. I read the reviews on Yelp all the time, and I really take them seriously," he added.

Kitchen staff meetings help Chef André and his two executive sous chefs keep everyone informed about critical particulars such as ingredients, presentation, and timing.

Some of the hundred-member kitchen staff who create Joe's memorable meals day in and day out.

While Chef André's purview is Joe's Stone Crab in Miami, at least twice a year he visits their Chicago and Las Vegas locations. "They are different. Chicago has more meat eaters. Vegas has more of a tourism business. We do influence them, but each is unique on its own."

Before Joe's actually had its own home in Las Vegas, there was a blurb in *Variety*, the Bible of the entertainment industry, bringing a great deal of attention to Joe's Stone Crab. The year was 1972. The Hotel Frontier in Las Vegas had just discontinued entertainment in its cocktail lounge, leaving a large empty marquee. To fill the space, "Joe's Stone Crabs from Miami" was displayed on the sign. Stone crabs were flown in from Miami, of course. Apparently Las Vegas visitors seeking entertainment thrills and not aware of the Miami Beach restaurant thought that "stone" meant "rock," as in rock and roll, and calls flooded the switchboard asking what time the rock group from Florida would be performing!

Much of what Chef André has accomplished is in making the environment work for the servers. "But I did have to make everyone understand the philosophy behind such things as purchasing; where the ingredients are from; what it takes to serve the food hot; and how important the presentation is. I get the best of everything to use in the preparation of our food. Meats and fish are flown in daily, and our prices are still so very reasonable."

It's no secret that a couple can get in and out at Joe's for under $20. "That's the amazing thing about our menu. You can get a couple of sodas, the yummy bread basket, and two orders of fried chicken, which is amazing in itself. And people are happy and have stayed within budget."

More surprising is that twice a day every day, a complimentary meal is prepared for Joe's staff of nearly four hundred people. "You know, it is really amazing. We spend over $35,000 every month on those meals alone. We have a rotating menu I've created that offers the staff the ability to get together and talk over problems, concerns, and the like, while they are tasting any new items we may have on the menu or learning about the day's specials. We talk about where all the food comes from. There is an interesting story behind every single product we use in the kitchen and about every item we sell. And it's the waiters who offer these fun and diverse and entertaining stories to our guests. These family meals that occur before every lunch and dinner really are important to the success of each of Joe's waiters."

The chef explained the philosophy in giving the waiters an hour-long paid break during their shifts. "They are our key salespeople. The fast pace here at Joe's is demanding. They need to relax and enjoy themselves too. And I'm sure they do. But they take their jobs seriously. They treat their little section of the restaurant as if it were their own special business, and they make it their own. That is part of their success as well as ours."

The twice daily family meals for Joe's nearly four hundred employees not only give staff first-hand knowledge of daily specials and new dishes but also build camaraderie.

A proud father of two, he beamed when recounting that his brilliant twenty-year-old son had decided to forgo aeronautical engineering and join him in the kitchen.

"He's always been so smart," Chef André observed. "And after working with me over the past few years, he decided that he also wants to be a chef. I am so proud. And I know that because of his background and his interests, he will approach this world quite differently than I do. I look forward to that."

Believe it or not, the chef's part-time hockey coaching gig has aided him in the kitchen. "I look at our kitchen staff as a team. We work together with a team effort approach to everything we do. We are a strong team that runs as one, and this has allowed Joe's to grow and expand greatly. That's what it takes to win."

The kitchen at Joe's is wide open. There are no doors separating the kitchen from the dining room. There are no secrets. There are no computerized orders. Every food request is handwritten by the waiters. These are handed to the two conductors, who are Joe's expeditors and who manipulate the kitchen with orchestra-like precision. These conductors, or sous chefs, know each waiter personally. They understand who may be fast, who is slow, whose handwriting is messy, and every meal is prepared within minutes, no matter what.

"It is vital that the waiters get through that first turn of their tables as quickly as possible. It sets the tone for the rest of the night," the chef continued. "Here in the kitchen, it is all about the waiters. It's all about making their job smoother, and easier, and faster. Of course, once the food is ready to leave the kitchen, it is checked again before landing on the tables.

"It's all about creating the very best team we can," Chef André continued as we stood in his kitchen at Joe's, watching the precise ballet of food preparation that takes place daily.

Joe's guests are paraded right by the open kitchen as they are led to their seats. And the kitchen that feeds more than fourteen hundred hungry customers every day runs as an amazingly smooth operation: "We've created what I call organized chaos here in Joe's kitchen, and it works," Chef André explained, echoing Beverage Director Paul Kozolis's description of it all as controlled chaos.

"And by the way, all of my cooks today were dishwashers first. We all believe in promotion here at Joe's. We've given people new careers and new opportunities," the chef proudly added.

Chef André and Stephen and Jo Ann make it a point to welcome their competition. "We are always nice to our neighbors. We go over and welcome them, and tell them, just like any good neighbor, that we are here if they need anything—to borrow

Astute attention from staff and orchestra-like precision from expeditors keep the kitchen ballet in step when service is at peak flow.

linens, or if they run out of something. That's always been the Joe's philosophy."

And while other restaurants come and go south of 5th Street in Miami Beach, Joe's isn't going anywhere. Another restaurant may charge four times what Joe's charges for mussels, for example, but it may also go under after a year or so. "You need to understand that high prices aren't what make for a successful restaurant," the chef explained. Joe's has certainly found a winning formula. Joe's is Joe's!

35

Jo Ann Weiss Sawitz Bass

"My grandfather, Joe Weiss, died before I was born. He was only sixty-eight. His wife, my grandmother Jennie, raised me pretty much all alone until I was seven years old, when she passed away," Jo Ann explained.

The tough, hardworking Jennie was seventy when she died. "Grandpa Joe, I am told, had asthma, which was why they came down to Florida in the first place," Jo Ann recalled. "And Jennie was obese and a diabetic. Over and over and over again, she would beg me to go to buy her candy, while I was simultaneously picking up her insulin!"

Jo Ann's parents, Frances and Jesse Weiss, were both just nineteen when they married, while Jesse was in college. Jesse was twenty-four when their only child was born. Frances passed away at twenty-six. Jesse was a gambler. He wasn't around much for the first years of his daughter's life. Jo Ann was raised by her paternal grandmother Jennie.

"But my grandmother wasn't around much either. Rather, let me say that she just wasn't very accessible. Her life was the restaurant. Honestly, I can say that the kitchen staff raised me. And Dad didn't like to work, so he wasn't around much back then. Jennie ran the show. Dad barely knew where the kitchen was.

"I wasn't an easy kid," Jo Ann reminisced. "I was an animal. I didn't have a mother. Dad wasn't around. Grandmother was too sick or too busy. She had such a terrible Hungarian temper. I was miserable with the situation. Grandmother was miserable with the situation."

Jennie and Jo Ann made some special adaptations, according to Grace Weiss, Jesse Weiss's fifth and seventh and final wife, who became Jo Ann's mother when the little girl was ten. "Jennie couldn't handle having a child. So she'd lock Jo Ann in the bathroom in the morning, and Jo Ann would climb out the window and go about her way, and then she'd climb back in at the end of the day." Jennie didn't seem to know.

"Jo Ann's life back then wasn't easy," Grace continued. "She had so many mothers and a grandmother who took no interest in the little girl at all."

The young Jo Ann lived over the store, above Joe's, with her grandmother, in the apartment that was built for the family. It overlooked the entire dining room of the building that was and is Joe's. "There were benefits to that," Jo Ann noted. "If I needed to be with my grandmother, or my dad, I just had to go downstairs."

It was Joe's, however, that Jo Ann considers her real parent. "Joe's brought me up. Especially our two chefs, Horatio "Rabbi" Johnson—we called him Rabbi because he would constantly mimic my grandmother's heavy Hungarian Jewish accent—and Benson "Seabreeze" Gardner.

"Grandpa Joe, I am told, met Benson on a beach. Joe asked how he was feeling, and he answered, 'I'm feeling the Seabreeze,' and Joe took a liking to him and offered him a job on the spot."

Both Rabbi and Seabreeze worked for Joe's for fifty years, and Jo Ann believes it is because of these two dear men that she began to consider the Joe's family her real family. "It was the kitchen staff who taught me everything. They nurtured me. They mothered me. I've always been connected to the people who work at Joe's because it is really all I've ever known."

Jo Ann's maternal grandfather Harry Levitt was the builder

Jo Ann Weiss Sawitz Bass attests to the fact that she was raised by the Joe's extended family, and she maintains the traditions of personal management, spontaneous acts of generosity, and investment in people.

of the original Joe's and of numerous other local establishments of the era. The Levitt side of the family had money, unlike Joe and Jennie Weiss, who put every dime they made back into the restaurant, while their only son Jesse would spend every cent he could on gambling.

"It was a constant battle," Jo Ann explained. "When my parents would get into financial trouble they'd go to Grandpa Levitt and he'd give them the money, but he'd only help out because of me. I was the apple of his eye.

"I was ten when Dad married Grace. She was just twenty-seven," Jo Ann recounted; still vibrant and active, Grace celebrated her ninety-eighth birthday as this book was being assembled.

"One of the first things Mother [Grace] and I did together was to go to meet every creditor in the area. We met with everyone to whom Dad owed money. We pleaded and begged and asked them to give Joe's another chance. Here we were, a cocky, naïve child of eleven and a beautiful twenty-eight-year-old woman. It must have been a funny sight, and we must have been convincing, because they did all eventually surrender."

Grace confirmed this: "Jo Ann and I were really just two kids. I had a bushel basket filled with so many bills. It took us ten years, but we paid every single one of them. Jesse's previous wife left the restaurant in such poor condition. Joe's was closed over the summer, as usual. A divorce occurred, and when I walked in for the first time as the new Mrs. Weiss, food from six months earlier was still on the stove. Jesse's ex-wife had left us with just six coffee cups. The place was a mess!"

Grace became a savior to Joe's and to Jo Ann, and has been there for them both ever since. "I truly believe that she is responsible for turning Joe's around," Jo Ann added.

"Grace and I just wouldn't give up," Jo Ann explained. "We fought so hard. I didn't have a lot of security growing up, but I always knew that if I had that building around me, that building called Joe's, that I'd have a place to sleep and food to eat."

When Jo Ann was about sixteen her parents again asked Harry Levitt for money. "This time Grandpa Levitt changed his tune a bit, however. He said that the only way he'd give them any more money was if they gave me half ownership in Joe's."

Jesse Weiss was eighty-seven when he died. Sadly, he lived the last twelve years of his life with Alzheimer's. "Everyone loved Jesse because he was a character. He was the official host of Joe's, a storyteller, a larger than life figure," his only daughter explained.

Fourth-generation Jodi Sawitz Hershey knows how deep the family values at Joe's run, from admiring the leadership of her mother Jo Ann to watching her granddaughter Alexandria grow up in the rhythms of her family's involvement with the restaurant.

Today Jo Ann is president of Joe's Stone Crab and her son Stephen Sawitz is the COO. "I worry about making sure I am guiding Stephen the right way, that he knows how to make the right decisions for the future of our family, the Joe's family," Jo Ann acknowledged. "The fact that we've helped so many of our family make decent lives for themselves, buy homes, send their kids to college—that makes me happy. I know Stephen will continue that tradition.

"Stephen is so fair in all of his thinking," his mother added. "He has an innate way of being there and putting his finger on the right thing." And of course, Stephen too was raised knowing the Joe's extended family as his own family.

Jo Ann's daughter Jodi offered some perspectives about what she and her brother learned from their mother: "Jo Ann is extremely loving and giving. She is so very much into taking care of others. She raised Stephen and me with tremendous values. We were all privileged to be able to watch others' lives

Larry King, seen with author Deeny Kaplan Lorber, has been in the Joe's orbit for more than fifty years. His radio career began in Miami Beach in 1957, and he was the announcer at the Miami Beach Dog Track next door to Joe's.

being transformed because of Joe's. Being a part of both families, Joe's and my own, has been such a gift."

Jo Ann was taken aback when asked what she would tell Joe and Jennie if she had the chance to show them around the restaurant today. "I wonder what they'd think of what we all created? I never knew Joe Weiss, my grandfather," Jo Ann pointed out. "My grandmother wasn't an easy woman to know. But if I had an afternoon to show them around today, I'd hope they would both be proud. I'd ask them if I was doing it right.

"The fact that we are able to give some 400 people and their families a decent life is something to be really proud of.

I think that is actually what I am the most proud of," Jo Ann concluded. "I would hope that they'd be as proud of what we've accomplished, thanks to their dream and hard work."

The very fact that the average Joe's employee has a twenty-five-year history with the establishment is certainly something special. Such employee longevity is rare in a business of any kind, let alone a restaurant. What Jo Ann and her family and extended family have created is truly something to be envied and emulated. As Larry King says, "there will never be another Joe's."

Jo Ann, of course, is a veritable fountain of information and knowledge in every aspect of the restaurant's operations, small and large. She observed, for example, that Joe's used to have cloth bibs. "I still have some of them. We would have our good customers' names embroidered on them and wash them and get them ready for the next time they'd come for dinner. We had a large iron mangle on the porch to press the cloth, and the names of these regular customers had been embroidered on the front. My grandmother actually did that. I think it was my mother, Grace, who switched us over to paper."

Jo Ann on tuxedos: "I don't ever remember the waiters wearing anything other than tuxedos. No one actually knows how the wearing of tuxedos by the waiters at Joe's got started. It could have been to emulate the old European style of service, which would have been formalwear."

On public figures: She said she loved J. Edgar Hoover. "He was always nice and took the time to talk with me, both as a little girl and into my later life. Today I'm sure we would have many disagreements politically.

"I never met Debbie Reynolds, but I was told that one night she was eating at Joe's for dinner. It grew late and she told the staff that she wanted them to go home, that they worked too hard and they needed to go home to spend time with their families. That was just so very thoughtful. I'll never forget that."

Her favorite celebrity? "Ann-Margret, she's my favorite. We met at the restaurant. She had a hard life, with many different situations, yet she was always up and there was always a smile on her face, and she always had something nice to say about everyone. She told me that if she were to tell someone they looked well, she knew that it would make their day, and that would make her happy. I really like her philosophy of life." Indeed, it closely mirrors Jo Ann's own always positive outlook.

36

STEPHEN SAWITZ

COO Stephen Sawitz first peeled shrimp and potatoes in Joe's kitchen when he was only eight or nine. "I wanted to make some money to buy a bike," Stephen recalled, "and it was also an opportunity for me to spend more time with my grandparents. They lived upstairs at the time.

"Joe's was never just a restaurant to me. It was the home of my grandparents, Jesse and Grace," Stephen added. From that home, high above the crab kingdom that is Joe's, you can see everything going on in Joe's dining room. The executive offices occupy that space today. Jo Ann Weiss Sawitz Bass has her office in what was once her family's kitchen.

Stephen's waiting days began in the Catskills while he was in college at Cornell, and according to the fourth-generation family heir, he learned a good deal there. He took to heart a remark by well-known chef and restaurateur Drew Nieporent, who also attended Cornell: "'Great actors take direction well. Servers are frustrated actors.' It's always on the tip of my tongue. And it's probably why each waiter is truly a performer, waiting for the applause, with a new show and a new audience to please, at least three times a night here at Joe's."

When Stephen Sawitz was sixteen he got his first car. His parents, Jo Ann and Irwin Sawitz, told him that since he was old enough to drive, he would have to learn responsibility. He was required to work at Joe's one day every week for the seven

Fourth-generation restaurateur Stephen Sawitz first started helping in the kitchen at age eight and today is Joe's chief operating officer.

months that Joe's would be open. "And I loved it. I did everything that Calvin Keel would ask me to do," Stephen added.

His favorite job? Working in the pantry. The young Stephen would clean the pantry, set it up, whip the cream, cut the pies, slice the bread, fill in utensils that were needed, and make the cheese balls and syrups. "It taught me a lot."

In college the young would-be restaurateur majored in hotel and restaurant management. The native Miamian was not at all happy with the cold and snowy winters of Ithaca, New York. When he returned to Miami after graduation, Joe's was closed for the summer, so he had to work elsewhere. His first job was with a local catering company. He'd work the kitchen, prepping and serving and transporting the food.

On Monday, November 4, 1979, the Iran hostage crisis began. Stephen remembers the date because it was the very next day that he began working full-time at Joe's: "I went overnight from catering for someone else to running lunch at my family's restaurant, and this was our very first season for lunch."

He hired the new lunch crew, for both the front and back of the house; introduced the lunchtime employee meal; and ordered the liquor. He would meet and greet and seat his guests. "It was overwhelming at first," Stephen attested. "I had to learn to delegate. I had to grow up fast.

"Calvin Keel, he was Superman," Stephen smiled, recalling the respect he had for his mentor. "He was old school all the way. In fifty years at Joe's, he missed only one day of work, when his son-in-law [who also worked at Joe's] passed away. Calvin started out bussing tables, and at the end he was senior manager for the entire restaurant.

"I know that when I began here, Calvin was a bit intimidated by me. I told him that he was a lifer at Joe's and that I was the one who was intimidated. I told him he could write his own ticket. I told him that I was in awe of him! Calvin set the tone for everything that goes on here. Calvin passed away in '08 and he is still very much missed by all of us."

Stephen looks out over the dining room. From working in the pantry to carrying stone crabs to the White House personally, he loves being immersed in the day-to-day action of Joe's.

The secret of Joe's key lime pie can be attributed directly to Jo Ann Weiss Sawitz Bass—the recipe is hers. "My mom is a great cook and an amazing baker," said Stephen. Jo Ann admitted to being happiest in the kitchen, attributing this to her grandmother Jennie—perhaps one of the few things the two had in common.

For the astoundingly long span of 1956 to 1995 Paul Wilson made the key lime pies for Joe's, using Jo Ann's recipe. "One day Paul went to take a nap on his cot in the back of the kitchen," Stephen recalled, "and he died right there, in his sleep, on that cot."

Jo Ann was away, Stephen added. "My mom was on a cruise, so I quickly counted the number of pies he had completed to see if we had enough to last until Mom returned. I counted and calculated and somehow I knew we'd make it. Mom got off the boat in the Port of Miami, and when I told her what had happened, she didn't miss a beat and went straight to the kitchen. She was upset about Paul, of course, but was such a trooper and got right to baking more key lime pies. The result: we were not short for even one meal."

What would have happened otherwise? "If we hadn't had enough pies until Mom came back, I would have made them," Stephen shared. "Mom taught me well. It's in my blood."

For the first and only time ever, Joe's closed its doors during lunch on the Saturday when Paul Wilson was buried. Florida's governor Bob Graham and his wife, huge fans of Paul's, attended the service. As far as Jo Ann could remember, "We didn't even close when my grandmother died." Larry Fisher then took over for Paul Wilson and has been the key lime king ever since.

If Stephen had a day to spend with his great-grandparents, Joe and Jennie Weiss, he said he would take them for a ride over the causeway that wasn't there a hundred years ago. "I'd tell them to look in the rearview mirror. I think they would be shocked. I'd tell them to put on their walking shoes so that I could show them around Joe's today—and I'd keep thanking them and thanking them." Stephen's eyes began to well up.

He loved his grandfather Jesse. "I would do everything I could to be with him. I never said no to him. He was a bit of a gambler. Everyone knows that. We had to keep his hand out of the till more than once. I think my parents can really be credited with making Joe's the financial success it is today," Stephen added.

"My favorite Joe's guest," Stephen reflected, "was Coretta Scott King. I had her sign a menu to the Joe's family. She was awesome. And there was Sandra Day O'Connor, Chief Justice Warren Burger, Billy Joel—I knew Billy was coming in, and being such a huge fan of his, I brought in all of my albums of his, every single one, and he signed them all."

Joe's provided Stephen with a most memorable personal adventure in 1996. "Florida governor Chiles's office called. They were going to the White House and were preparing to announce that the Summit of the Americas would be convening in Miami. The governor wanted to bring stone crabs from Joe's to the event. I asked when, and they said, right now, get on the next plane. I took them seriously, packed a bag, left food out for my cat, had the stone crabs prepared and packed them in ice, and left on the next flight to D.C. While I was moving through first class, one of the passengers saw the familiar Joe's Stone Crab box and asked me how much I wanted for them. I answered, 'Sir, there is no amount of money in the world that you could offer me to buy these stone crabs.' Little did he know they were for President Clinton. I tell you, that box didn't leave my side until it got safely to the White House!"

37

GRACE WEISS

Jo Ann refers to Grace Weiss as Mother. To Stephen Sawitz and his sister Jodi, she is Sweetie. This year Grace is ninety-eight, just a touch younger than Joe's Stone Crab, and certainly not your typical ninety-eight-year-old woman. She retired when she was seventy but still visits frequently from her home in North Carolina and takes pride in what her family has accomplished.

Grace was Jesse Weiss's fifth and seventh and last wife. She is tough but definitely has a soft side, as all who know her agree.

"Grace was still working in the office when I started at Joe's back in 1979," explained Paul Kozolis, beverage director for the establishment. "She is very straightforward. Grace was in charge of the registers back then. And while Grace was tough and regimented about money, her husband Jesse was just the opposite," Paul continued. "Jesse would come up to my register—I was a bartender back then—and say, 'Hey kid, give me $500!' He didn't even think about the fact that I was responsible for my register. He'd also go right over to the tables and grab the checks before the waiters did and pocket the cash. Of course, he used the cash across the street, at the track."

Grace enjoyed being a resident: "We lived upstairs from the dining room at Joe's, where Jesse's parents used to live. I never met them, but I've heard all of the stories. You could see

Called Mother by Jo Ann and Sweetie by Jodi and Stephen, Grace Weiss is the family's grand matriarch at ninety-eight years young. Now retired from Joe's and living in North Carolina, she revels in memories of the great parties at Joe's in midcentury. She is also quietly acknowledged as the determined woman who steered Joe's out of debt during that same period.

everything from our window. I'd even catch some of the waiters smoking in the alley."

Although she still frequently visits Joe's, she won't go back upstairs. "No, I haven't been back since I retired," she affirmed. "I just don't want to. There are too many memories. But living upstairs from the restaurant had its perks. I was like Mrs. Macy. I lived above the store and loved it."

Although her husband Jesse was regarded as the gambler in the Weiss family, Grace is somewhat of a gambler herself. A Colorado native, she had plans to be an artist, to be in show business. She wanted an exciting, theatrical, glamorous type of life.

Grace met Jesse when he was in the army, in Chicago. "He was dangerously exciting," she admitted. "Jesse knew every hoodlum and café owner in town. We went everywhere for free. Everywhere. We didn't pay for anything. We truly were what you would call America's guests!

"I could have married into show biz," Grace explained. "But something pulled me to this little girl who needed a mother. I knew where I was needed. And I have absolutely no regrets whatsoever."

When Grace first came to Joe's, there was one telephone. "It was an old wooden phone booth, and I would stand in it every morning and place our food orders. There was no other place to order and no place to sit. Today, Joe's has over sixty phones. Times sure have changed! But something we will never have here would be the automated answering machines most businesses use today. Never at Joe's. When you call us, there is always a person willing to help on the other end of the phone. That has always been our philosophy."

She reflected on the staff. "We've had so many great waiters at Joe's. One of my favorites was a guy named Fred. He was a wonderful man. He was very British, from London. You know, very proper. On his day off he'd be at home, and he'd put the candles, the silver, and a tablecloth on the table, and another set of the same on the floor. The settings were beautiful. And Fred and his dog would eat royally. The same way, every week.

"And the same waiter, Fred, who had been with us for nearly forty years, he was funny. Once Fred had a very fussy woman customer who started complaining about her food. There really wasn't anything wrong with it, and Fred knew that. He came to her pleading, 'Please don't say anything. This is my first day. I don't want to get fired on my first day. I need the job!' Of course it wasn't really his first day, and the woman did finish her meal and didn't say a word. He had that very British charm about him.

"Our kitchen staff has always been on the ball as well," Grace recalled. "In the early days we had one automatic dishwasher, and one day it broke. One of the kitchen staff, a young man named Valation Gray who couldn't even write his own name, fixed that dishwasher with a coat hanger, and we didn't know what he'd done until after the dinner guests went home. No one had to stop or change routine. He did it on his own. He saved us from having to do all the dishes that night by hand."

She reminisced about some notable connections: "My choice was the right one. I still had my fill of show biz and exciting times. Joe's has given me that. J. Edgar Hoover was a very dear friend. So was [columnist and broadcaster] Walter Winchell, and Larry King called me on my ninetieth birthday! He is still a good friend.

"One night Jimmy Stewart and Henry Fonda were at a table for six. Both of them had pacemakers on at the time. Our friendship went way back. I knew them both when they were young boys, but those are the type of customers we had," Grace explained. "Every night was a party, and you never knew what celebrity would walk in."

Jesse wanted to be at Joe's only when there was action. He was a showman. Waiting on tables wasn't for him. But Jesse Weiss did start out working on the porch of his parents' small fish restaurant. "Waiting tables in those days was when a young Jesse Weiss met the thugs in town—and they were lifelong Joe's fans.

"Joe's will be here in another hundred years," Grace Weiss proclaimed. "Our people always train the next generation. Jo Ann took up where I left off. She's so bright and always calm. She works very hard. Stephen is such a wonderful young man. Both of them are amazing! My granddaughter Jodi's son-in-law Jose, he's a gifted young man too, and he's working at Joe's. Together they will see the restaurant continue to grow and prosper."

Grace prophesied that a hundred years from now, "we'll have the next generations of our family and our extended family getting ready to celebrate the two-hundredth anniversary of Joe's Stone Crab."

Will there still be stone crabs? No need to worry. Females

The view onto the dining room from the Weiss family's original apartment.

produce between half a million and a million eggs, four to six times during the summer spawning season, every year.

Stone Crab claws grow back in about a year, typically larger than before. The harvesting at the two Joe's fisheries is a process that removes both claws from the live animal, which then regrows the lost limbs. Certain measurements must be met in order for the claws to be harvested: they must measure at least 2.75 inches long from the tip of the immovable finger to the first joint.

And of course, the stone crab season, as any regular Joe's customer knows, is only from October 15 until May 15.

EPITAPH

The ultimate allegiance to Joe's Stone Crab is hands down the story of Phil Grier, who had always said he had wanted to be buried at the restaurant he called home. At the age of eighty, the retired seventeen-year veteran Joe's waiter did come home.

Phil had left the restaurant to retire in 1987. One day in 1996 he showed up again, only this time he was in a box—well, his ashes were delivered in a box—and sure enough, the entire staff held a grand ceremony and buried Phil's ashes in the garden, in the front of Joe's front bar, just the way Phil wanted. There's been a small memorial plaque in the garden ever since, and more than a decade later Joe's waiters continue to acknowledge Phil's presence and his commitment to the restaurant he loved.

Rose McDaniel, Joe's dining room manager then and now, says, "Phil's not alone in his thoughts. I want to be buried there too." And Rose is not kidding.

Others have followed Phil's lead: well-known Miami broadcaster Ann Bishop, who was a dear friend of the Weiss family; Dr. Bob Bass, Jo Ann's husband; and Mike Boro—a loyal Joe's customer. (No regulation prohibits these burials at Joe's.)

Another patron who was a long-time fan of Joe's was Charles Frederick Sharp, former president and owner of Woodlawn Park Cemetery in Miami. Charles passed away in 1993. The inscription on his tombstone at his mausoleum crypt in the Wood-

After retiring as a waiter in 1987, Phil Grier wanted to return in perpetuity—and so he did in 1996, when his ashes were interred in the garden at the front of the restaurant, inspiring a continuing trend among Joe's family, friends, and customers. Joe's is clearly worth the wait!

lawn Park Cemetery reads: "I'd rather be at Joe's!"—rendered in the iconic style of the authentic Joe's logo.

Apparently when Charles first fell ill, he told his family that he wasn't enjoying himself and he'd rather be at Joe's. It became something of a joke, and then it became a reality. Now that's eternal loyalty.

Yes, waiting at Joe's has its perks. Who knew it was an eternity of perks?

Joe's Stone Crab has been and is now a true family. May it continue to be so for generations to come.

ACKNOWLEDGMENTS

Thank you to the Joe's family: Jo Ann Weiss Sawitz Bass, Stephen Sawitz, Jodi Sawitz Hershey, Grace Weiss, Ed Witte, Jose Uchuya, and Brian Johnson. Thanks to the amazing Joe's team, whose enthusiasm and encouragement were constant, as well as to the folks behind the scenes there, including: Karl "Chopper" Robertson, Luis Rosales, Marc Fine, Rose McDaniel, Paul Kozolis, and Lori Kahn.

And of course, my love and special thanks to my own personal team of cheerleaders: Ken, Adam, Max, and Sheridan Lorber and my parents, Hike and Herman Kaplan.

In dedicating this book to my nephew, Adam Balzano, I wanted to share one of my last memories of Adam, which is also one of my favorite Joe's stories.

Adam was a handsome, talented, wonderful young man who got very sick. We knew he didn't have much time left, and I asked his mother, Rhea, what we could do for him. At that point Adam could barely speak, but he somehow managed to tell his mother that he wanted Joe's stone crab and everything that came with it.

Adam lived in Brooklyn Heights, New York. We would have to ship the dinner. One Tuesday night I was with some friends having dinner at Joe's. Jo Ann happened to be there. I told her about Adam and that I'd be back over the weekend to buy the dinner, which would most likely be his last supper.

Without hesitation Jo Ann grabbed my hand and led me to the kitchen. She asked for Adam's address and proceeded to place an order that would have been enough for a family of four.

She told me that from what I had told her, Adam wouldn't make it to the weekend. And she wouldn't take any money. Right then and there, without a moment's hesitation, she shipped Adam a veritable Joe's feast.

The next evening my sister-in-law called me and spoke on Adam's behalf. He couldn't talk any more. But he did eat his Joe's supper, all of it. There was even a smile on his face, in a beautiful body filled with pain.

That night Adam passed away. It *was* his last supper. It's a bittersweet story. Jo Ann was right. Had I waited for the weekend, I would have missed my last chance to reach out to Adam.

This book is my very special birthday gift to Joe's Stone Crab and my thank you to Jo Ann Weiss Sawitz Bass for her generosity. It is my own special Joe's story. But I must tell you that after interviewing more than fifty Joe's employees, it seems that everyone else has a similar Jo Ann story!

DEENY KAPLAN LORBER is a founding partner and executive vice president of the primetime Emmy® Award winning TM Systems and its language services division, The Kitchen, one of the entertainment industry's most respected language dubbing companies, based in Miami and Los Angeles. With a radio, television, publishing, production, and post-production industry background that started at the ripe old age of 12, Deeny Kaplan Lorber continues to explore new depths in a business she adores. *Waiting at Joe's* is her first book.